Your Fresh Start

by Cindy Dunagan

"...times of refreshing may come from the presence of the Lord..."

—Acts 3:19 (NKJV)

"...anyone who belongs to Christ has become a new person. The old life is gone; a new life has begun!"

—2 Corinthians 5:17 (NLT)

ONE STONE
BIBLICAL RESOURCES

Published by:
One Stone Press
979 Lovers Lane
Bowling Green, KY 42103

Printed in the United States of America

ISBN 13: 978-1-941422-29-8

ONE STONE
BIBLICAL RESOURCES

www.onestone.com

Table of Contents

Introduction

The book you now hold in your hand has been around the block. Soon after writing it, my sister in Christ and I prayed that God would grant us opportunities to shine His light and that He'd make fruitful our labors. Then we packed to the hilt my silver FJ Cruiser with copies of *Your Fresh Start*, about 30 donated Bibles, and everything else it takes to live on the road for 8 weeks. My husband of 38 years kissed me goodbye and we empty nesters began our unforgettable journey.

Within just 90 minutes driving west up Hwy. 26, we parked and hiked to the top of icy Saddle Mountain in Oregon's lush Tillamook Forest. There we met a Jewish woman from England named Lisa. When she asked who we were and what we were up to, we explained how we were combining some grand adventuring and sharing God with whomever He put in our path. Her jaw dropped, she poured out her heart's burdens to us and we prayed together atop that gorgeous 3,290' summit. Lisa listened attentively on our descent to the Biblical evidences for Jesus being the Messiah and gratefully received the first copy we distributed on our road trip of *Your Fresh Start* containing those evidences in written form. It was amazing.

I could write a book of full of God's providence during those 57 days my three brave travelling companions and I journeyed 11,300 miles from Kirkland, Washington, south to Palm Springs, east to Tampa, north to Boston and west back to my home in Beaverton, Oregon. You'd hear about volunteers at a church of Christ helping prepare the 30 donated Bibles for distribution by highlighting key verses, inserting lovely homemade bookmarks and a note I'd written, then the next day packed lunches for Seattle's homeless complete with pocket-size Bibles. They also put soul-saving scripture stickers on the back of our little black and white "Only God" 2" x 3" cards that we left for strangers to discover everywhere from the steps of the Supreme Court to Niagara Falls to Bourbon Street to the Badlands, that souls might stop and think for a moment about the Creator and eternity.

If I told my story, you'd hear how within just a few hours a broken cell phone turned into an opportunity to study the Bible by firelight at my beach house with a lovely, open-hearted Peruvian woman. How when I handed a free Bible to a young female tourist from China I'd connected with on the Staten Island Ferry touring the Statue of Liberty she asked if the title "Holy Bible" was someone's name—so foreign this life-changing book was to her. I explained slowly, pointing heavenward, "No. It is God talking to people."

I'd love to tell you the detailed story of leaving behind a copy of *Your Fresh Start* with some empty nesters who had housed me in Lyons, New York, then 20 minutes after saying our goodbyes, my being invited to sit with some other strangers to eat breakfast at McDonald's—strangers who just happened to know my hosts from the night before, because my hosts' son had plowed into their car while learning to drive years earlier. "Nice people," they recalled. After a good, long talk, I gifted them some of my sparkly little bohemian art trinkets as they left the parking lot and texted my hosts, "I think these regulars at McDonald's down the street would be open to a Bible study," using God's providence to do a little spiritual match making.

One of our last nights on the road, we were being hosted in Missoula, Montana by a sweet sister in Christ who was a friend of a friend. As we were getting settled for the night I heard my friend say loudly from the other room "Wait. *Your* maiden name is...?! I prayed *ten years* for you!" My traveling companion's prayers that the little girl she had never met would survive her life-threatening childhood illness had been answered. In fact, by God's providence, she got to hold in her arms the beautiful little boy that was the result of God's divine mercy.

My brave soul sisters Stephanie Merrill, Rhonda Ray Clark, and Deb McCown tag-teamed travelling with me through 30 states. We toured the inside of the White House and did a little couch surfing, soaking up all manner of warm hospitality from 31 open-hearted hosts who'd pray aloud with us upon our parting those wonderful 57 days we handed out copies of *Your Fresh Start*. I learned a lot on the "Only God" road trip. I learned how incredibly hospitable to strangers the church of Christ is—that a simple shout out on Facebook would over and over again lead to an offer of hospitality from a friend of a friend. I learned that sharing God's truths is easier than we think and that we do best to just relax. Seriously. Conversations will flow naturally. I learned that if we choose to be our most confident, warm, natural, engaging self and think happy thoughts (Phil. 4:8) connecting with people in deep, spiritually meaningful ways is incredibly fulfilling and fun. To offer someone a *fresh start* is better than throwing diamonds at their feet, and most people realize we are loving them when we share truth.

I encourage you to keep your backpack stocked with a Bible, perhaps a copy of *Your Fresh Start* or whatever you like better, and *ask God* for fearlessness, opportunities and the right words, then stand back and be amazed at what He through His providence accomplishes. Hallelujah.

Lesson 1

Behold Thy God

Most of us may live in this beautiful world about 80 years. Seems like a long time. But when you think about it, eternity is like endless miles of sand dunes, and our life span is in comparison like a single grain of sand. If it is true that virtually all of our existence will be spent in the next world, and if it is true that the quality of our future existence is based upon choices we make in this life, the only wise thing to do is to carefully prepare for that eternity. Mortality... it's not the easiest thing to ponder. In fact, most of us immerse ourselves in an almost frantic level of activity in an effort to avoid thinking about the inevitable. But hey, I get that. I love this life too! I love spending my life with the man I love, watching the joy in our children as they learn and discover exciting, new things. I love the smell of the beach and walking through the woods in the spring. I love laughing with my friends, and I truly love my work. Yet even life at its best leaves us wanting more. Is there more? Is there life after death? Is there a God? If so, what are His expectations of me? These are the real questions of life that those who are courageous and honest enough must slow down from their very full and busy lives long enough to answer. In the course of preparing for eternity, the changes of doing so has ripple effects that often multiply the enjoyment we get out of this life.

Why do I, and a very high percentage of people in this world, acknowledge the existence of God? I mean, all day long most of those whom the world would identify as the intellectually elite preach the gospel of atheism. I say the *"gospel* of atheism" because essentially the message we as a culture are suppose to be embracing is, in essence, the message, "Lighten up. The evidence is in: we have

> For since the creation of the world His invisible attributes, His eternal power and divine nature, have been **clearly seen**, being understood through what has been made, so that they are without excuse.
>
> - Romans 1:20

proven yet again that there is no God. Live the way you like; if it feels good do it. There is no ultimate authority. And if you too want to be viewed as an intellectual, you too will preach this same good news." Yet after vast support of most media, much of the educational system, and everything in-between, most people *still* believe in a God. The truth is, atheists just can't preach a sermon as convincing as the awe-inspiring universe preaches every day. "For since the creation of the world His invisible attributes, His eternal power and divine nature, have been clearly seen, being understood through what has been made, so that they are without excuse" (Romans 1:20). How does one determine if there is a God? Think with me.

The Universe Exists

This fact alone forces us to confront the question, "Where did the universe originate?" Can something come from nothing? Ponder this: If there ever had been a time when nothing existed, then there would be nothing now. It is a self-evident truth that nothing produces nothing. In view of this, since something exists now, it must follow logically that something or Someone has existed forever. Here we only have two choices. Either everything miraculously came from nothing (life spontaneously generated), or God miraculously created everything (Genesis 1:1). Which miracle is most likely? Which miracle does the evidence support? Has matter existed forever or has immaterial intelligence existed forever? Matter creating matter is an illogical, unscientific answer; this is readily seen in the very fact that scientists assign an "age" to the universe (which includes all the matter that composes it). An age admits a "beginning" or starting point and proves that matter is not eternal. This universe that exists either came from mind, or it came from matter. When one explores the complexity and wise design of the universe, the only reasonable and scientific conclusion the honest mind can reach is that an omniscient mind with omniscient power has always existed.

In the beginning **God created** the heavens and the earth.

- Genesis 1:1

The First Cause

The scientific law of cause and effect states that every material effect must have an adequate cause. All that you see around you is an effect, but what is the cause? What caused our complex universe to exist? What caused intelligent life in nature to exist? Beyond the material, what caused man's moral nature, or his ability to love? What is the origin of the laws of nature? What is the origin of all truth, spirituality, and values? The explanation that best fits the scientific law of cause and effect is well stated by Dr. Henry Morris.

The first cause of limitless space
must be infinite

The first cause of endless time
must be eternal

The first cause of boundless energy
must be all-powerful

The first cause of universal interrelationships
must be omnipresent

The first cause of infinite complexity
must be all-knowing

The first cause of moral values
must be moral

The first cause of spiritual values
must be spiritual

The first cause of human responsibility
must have free will

The first cause of human integrity
must be truthful

The first cause of human love
must be loving

The first cause of life
must be living

Behold, thy God is the first cause of all that is good.

The scientific law of cause and effect states that every **material effect** must have an **adequate cause**.

Certainly the **design and care** with which the laws of physics, the universe, our galaxy, our solar system, and the planet Earth were crafted demands an **omniscient, omnipotent Creator**.

The Exacting Conditions for Life on the Planet are Anything But a Fluke

"For thus says the LORD, who created the heavens (He is the God who formed the earth and made it, He established it and did not create it a waste place, but formed it to be inhabited), 'I am the LORD, and there is none else' (Isaiah 45:18).

The countless exacting conditions that are necessary for life to even exist and be sustained on this planet shout the existence of an intelligent designer.

"The rotation of the earth on its axis, for instance, is 1,000 mile per hour at the equator. If it were 100 instead, the days and nights would be ten times as long, the result of which would be the burning up of all vegetation each long day and the freezing of each surviving sprout each long night. The sun, the source of light, has surface temperatures of 12,000 degrees Fahrenheit; the earth is far enough away for the right warmth, not too far, yet not too close. If the sun gave less radiation, the result would freeze us all, and if more, it would roast us all. The slant of the earth is at an angle of 23 degrees, which gives seasons, and if not so tilted, the movement of the vapors of the sea would turn continents into ice. If the moon were set at less distance from the earth, tides would submerge all continents twice daily and the mountains would erode away. If the crust of the earth were ten feet thicker, there would be no oxygen and all life would die, and if the ocean were a few feet deeper, no life could exist. If the atmosphere were thinner...meteors which hurl from their orbits and dart toward the earth and which now burn...in the atmosphere, would shoot to ground and set fires over the whole earth is proof that life was created, is governed by mathematical laws, and is not an accident." (*Bulwarks of the Faith, Vol. 11*, pages 332, 333. F.E. Wallace)

Certainly the design and care with which the laws of physics, the universe, our galaxy, our solar system, and the planet Earth were crafted demands an omniscient, omnipotent Creator.

The Human Body: Evidence of Ultra-Intelligent Design

"I will give thanks to Thee, for I am fearfully and wonderfully made" (Psalm 139:14).

- **The human eye.** Every single part of the body, down to the cellular level, is "...a masterpiece and mechanism of precise planning, a delicate and complex apparatus whose various components work as a unit to achieve such diverse feats as scaling a mountaintop, building a bridge or composing a symphony" (Nourse, Alan E., ed. 1964. *The Body*. New York: Time, Inc. Apologetics Press.org).

Consider the eye, for example. It is "infinitely more complex than any man-made camera. It can handle 1.5 million simultaneous messages, and gathers 80% of all the knowledge absorbed by the brain. The retina covers less than a square inch, and contains 137 million light-sensitive receptor cells, 130 million rods (allowing the eye to see in black and white), and 7 million cones (allowing the eye to see in full color). In an average day, the eye moves about 100,000 times..." (Thompson, Bert. *The Design Argument—"Eye" of the Storm*. Apologeticspress.org).

"The eye is still far superior to the best of modern cameras—it is much more sensitive than the fastest film, sees over a wide angle, presents a moving picture, cleans itself, is self-focusing, and has the remarkable property of remaining effective despite enormous changes in the intensity of illumination, adjusting to such changes automatically" (Clark, Robert E.D. *The Universe—Plan or Accident?* London: Paternoster. 1949, p. 150).

How do we answer for the existence of such a complicated and efficient instrument as the human eye? If someone handed us a digital camera, no honest and reasonable person could deny it had been designed and manufactured for a

> Consider the **eye**...It is infinitely **more complex** than any man-made camera.

purpose. How much more evident it is that such an infinitely more complex masterpiece as the human eye is obviously the work of the Ultimate Genius.

- **The human brain.** "The brain is a physical system that contains about 100 billion interconnected neurons—about as many neurons as there are stars in the Milky Way galaxy..." (Trefil, James. 1996. *101 Things You Don't Know About Science and No One Else Does Either.* Boston, MA: Houghton Mifflin. Apologeticspress. org. *The Origin of the Brain and Mind [Part I]*. Bert Thompson, Ph.D.; Brad Harrub, Ph.D).

> The more intelligent the **design**, the more intelligent the **designer**.

"The human brain weighs only about three pounds, yet contains ten billion neurons with approximately 25,000 synapses (connections) per neuron. Each neuron is made up of 10,000,000,000 macromolecules. The human mind can store almost limitless amounts of information" (Wysong, R.L. 1976. *The Creation-Evolution Controversy.* Midland, MI: Inquiry Press. Apologeticspress.org. *The Origin of the Brain and Mind [Part I]* Bert Thompson, Ph.D.; Brad Harrub, Ph.D.). It can compare facts, weigh information against memory, formulate a decision in a fraction of a second, make judgments, impart consciousness, and more. What honest person would say that your personal computer is an example of extraordinary planning and design, but the brain that engineered and produced the computer is just the product of blind chance? The more intelligent the design, the more intelligent the designer.

- **DNA.** Deoxyribonucleic acid is a molecule that carries the genetic instructions used in the growth, development, functioning and reproduction of all known living organisms and many viruses. In 2003, the final draft of the human genome was completed. DNA is referred to by scientists as the "blueprint" of life. It was discovered that if all the DNA in your body was put end to end, it would reach to the sun and back over 600 times (100 trillion times six feet divided by 92 million miles). It would take a person typing 60 words per minute, eight hours a day, around 50 years to type the human genome. If all three billion letters in the human genome were stacked one millimeter apart, they would reach a height 7,000 times the height of the Empire State Building. Our entire DNA sequence would fill 200 1,000-page New York City telephone directories. A complete 3 billion base genome would take 3 gigabytes of storage space. If unwound and tied together, the strands of DNA in one cell would stretch almost six feet but would be only 50 trillionths of an inch wide. In humans, the DNA molecule in a non-sex cell would have a total length of 1.7 meters. If you unwrap the DNA you have in all your cells, you could reach the moon 6000 times! If uncoiled, the DNA in all the cells in your body would stretch 10 billion miles—from here to Pluto and back. During the course of heading up the genome project, scientist Francis Collins went from atheist to believer because of the divine level of intelligent design he witnessed firsthand. As a result, he wrote a book that was an instant bestseller called *The Language of God*. It provided arguments for the integration of faith and logic that has led many modern day scientists to walk away from their preconceived ideas, toward a Divine Creator. Even the secular world has acknowledged the relevancy of his book: "Collins's argument that science and faith are compatible deserves a wide hearing. It lets non-churchgoers consider spiritual questions without feeling awkward" (*The New York Times* book review). "*The Language of God* is a powerful confession of belief from one of the world's leading scientists. Refuting the tired stereotypes of hostility between science and religion, Francis Collins challenges his readers to find a unity of knowledge that encompasses both faith and reason" (Kenneth Miller, Brown University,

A Creator with **infinite wisdom and power** is the only logical explanation for the existence of our **infinitely complex blueprint**.

> Then God said, "Let Us make man **in Our image**, according to Our likeness; let them have dominion over the fish of the sea, over the birds of the air, and over the cattle, over all the earth and over every creeping thing that creeps on the earth."
>
> - Genesis 1:26

author of *Finding Darwin's God*). No wonder this humble man came to his honest conclusion. Compare DNA, this so called "blueprint of life" or sometimes also called "instruction book of life" with a simple book for children. Do you believe a simple children's book about, say... animals could make itself? That all the colors can just fall from the sky out of nothing? That all the letters, given enough time, could fall perfectly into place to create this book? Then how much more unlikely is it that the real animals pictured in the book made up of a vastly more complex blueprint called DNA which is the written code for every cell of every living thing, a zillion times more complex than the child's book, make itself? A Creator with infinite wisdom and power is the only logical explanation for the existence of our infinitely complex blueprint.

The Spiritual Nature of Man

Our very moral nature is evidence that man is created in the image of God. Even atheists acknowledge right and wrong exist when they say such things as, "You shouldn't do that," or "That's not right." People are naturally outraged by evil, because evil exists and is naturally offensive. Of course if we are nothing but matter, we cannot be evil because matter cannot be evil; it is morally neutral. Also, evil cannot exist if there is no God. The reason why man is predisposed with a religious nature is because he was designed to worship his Creator. Every culture has worshiped or served someone or something (Acts 17:21). The existence of religion proves that man is so much more than a body and has an undeniable spiritual dimension. The fact that we have an intellect, a religious inclination, an aesthetic appreciation and a moral nature shows we have been created in the image of a complex God (Genesis 1:26).

The Unfathomable Size of the Universe

To say we live in an incredibly large universe is an understatement. While its outer limits have never been measured, it is estimated to be as much as 20 billion light years in diameter (a light year is the distance that light travels in a vacuum in one year at the speed of slightly more than 186,000 miles per second). Yet there are an estimated one billion galaxies in the universe. Our own galaxy contains over 100 billion stars and is so large that it would take 100,000 light years just to cross its diameter. It is unscientific to claim that a single light bulb happened by chance—how much more, a universe filled with matter that is 20 billion light years in diameter! There can be no other honest explanation for such vastness than an all-knowing, all-powerful, omnipresent God.

The Undeniable Conclusion

God exists. Both this astonishing universe and your very nature alone prove it.

The courageous mind must then ask, "Has God communicated with His creation, and if so, what has He said?" Even more significantly, "Has He expressed any expectations of me in my life?" Our next lesson in this series will address these most important questions of life.

As we conclude this lesson I would like to leave you with an introduction to the incomparable character of your awesome God. The three persons of the Godhead—the Father, Son and Holy Spirit—are said in scripture to be:

- Compassionate, gracious, slow to anger, abounding in lovingkindness, and forgiving (Exodus 34:6-7)

- The Creator, everlasting, inexhaustible, inscrutable understanding, giving (Isaiah 40:28-29)

- Faithful, and our provider (1 Corinthians 10:13)

..."The Lord, the Lord God, **merciful** and **gracious**, **longsuffering**, and abounding in **goodness** and **truth**, keeping **mercy** for thousands, **forgiving** iniquity and transgression and sin..."

- Exodus 34:6-7

- He is our Holy Father and impartial (1 Peter 1:14-17)

- God is good (Luke 18:19)

- He is our guide (Psalm 48:14)

- God is immutable—which means He does not change (Malachi 3:6)

- He is great, strong, and infinite (Psalm 147:5)

- He is our King, eternal, immortal, invisible (1 Timothy 1:17)

- Our God can be jealous, avenging, wrathful, yet slow to anger (Naham 1:2-3)

- He is righteous and just (Psalm 119:137)

- God is wise (Romans 16:27)

- Patient (2 Peter 3:9)

- Loving (1 John 4:8)

- Merciful (Ephesians 2:4-5)

- God is omnipresent, meaning He can be everywhere (1 Kings 8:27)

- God is omniscient, meaning He knows all (1 Chronicles 28:9)

- God is omnipotent, meaning He is all-powerful (Matthew 19:26)

- He is perfect (Matthew 5:48)

- He is our Savior (1 Timothy 4:10)

- God is self-existent (Revelation 22:13)

- He is the sovereign, or supreme ruler (1 Timothy 6:15-16)

- He is a spirit (John 4:24)

- God is our only source of all truth (Psalm 31:5)

Our God is an awesome God. We are promised that if we draw near to God, He will draw near to us (James 4:8). I prayerfully encourage you to begin drawing near to your awesome God today.

The Bible: God's Will Revealed

After examining the amazing order and design of the universe, considering how meticulously created our bodies are and taking into account our very spiritual nature, the most reasonable and honest explanation for all of this is that God undeniably exists, and He indeed *has* created all the physical things our five senses perceive.

This being true, the next logical question is: has God communicated with His creation, and if so, what has He said? What is God's purpose for creating us?

Not only is it possible God has communicated to His creation; it is also probable. It is illogical to think God would put all this planning and effort into creating man and then leave him without any instructions or guidance. Just as we want to be intimately involved with the children we bring into this world, it is natural that our heavenly Father would want to communicate with His creation and be lovingly attentive to those He has created.

God's communication with us is not only probable, it is necessary. The maker of a computer designs it for a specific purpose and writes programs and instructions in it to help it fulfill its intended purposes, functioning the way he intended. Just as those who created the computer communicate how to use it, so our Creator designed us for a specific purpose and has left instructions regarding how to fulfill these purposes.

The maker of a car builds it to certain specifications, including an operations manual to help properly care for and use the car. So also the Maker of mankind, having a purpose and plan in

> ...His divine power has given to us **all things that pertain to life and godliness**, through the knowledge of Him who called us by glory and virtue...
>
> - 2 Peter 1:3

mind for mankind, has left instructions so we can each reach our full potential (2 Peter 1:3; Psalm 119:97-105).

> The **heavens declare the glory of God**; And the firmament shows His handiwork.
>
> - Psalm 19:1

Although "the heavens declare the glory of God" (Psalm 19:1-4), it is impossible to fully know God's character, His purposes or His plans without more information than what we see in nature. As man observes all that has been created, he gets but a small glimpse of God's vast power and wisdom. The natural response by mankind is to worship such an awesome Creator (Acts 17:23). Without revelation from God to man, man by his own wisdom and resources, never fully knows the other qualities of God or His expectations for mankind (Jeremiah 10:23), or how He wants us to express our gratitude to Him. Without communication from God, you and I would be left to wonder why we were created, and why are we here on this planet.

The Bible claims to be God's instruction manual, God's revealing of His own desires for mankind (2 Timothy 3:16). In fact, in the Old Testament alone there are 2,700 statements that make a claim of inspiration. But is there evidence to support what the Bible claims? Is this book truly God's instruction manual for mankind? This lesson will examine the evidence that proves the Bible truly is God's word and is therefore worthy of the time it takes to read it, understand it and live by it.

Evidences of Inspiration

Pre-scientific foreknowledge

The Bible mentions many scientific truths long, long before man discovered such with his technology. This again proves God as the Bible's source.

1. The very first verse of the Bible states, "In the beginning God created the heavens and the earth" (Genesis 1:1). Modern science informs us that there are five forces necessary for existence. They are: time, energy, force, space, and matter. Is it mere coincidence that all these forces are

seen in the statement, "In the beginning God created the heaven and the earth"? There was time ("in the beginning"), energy ("God"), force ("created"), space ("heavens," ASV), and matter ("the earth").

2. Twice in the Bible, God said the earth is round. First, in about 1000 BC when He said, "From the beginning, from the earliest times of the earth... He inscribed *a circle* on the face of the deep..." (Proverbs 8:23, 27), and again about 700 years before Christ through the prophet Isaiah, "Do you not know? Have you not heard? Has it not been declared to you from the beginning? Have you not understood from the foundations of the earth? It is He who sits above *the circle of the earth*" (Isaiah 40:21-22). Beginning in about 1520, navigational instruments led to the gradual acceptance that the earth is spherical, over 2,500 years after God stated such! The Bible is from the God who created this great circle of the earth. The only way to account for such an old book knowing such a fact is because of its divine origin.

3. The First Law of Thermodynamics was confirmed by Sadi Carnot, referred to as "the father of thermodynamics." In 1824 he published *Reflections on the Motive Power of Fire*, marking the start of thermodynamics as a modern science. Simply put, this law states that no new matter is being created. Yet some 3,000 years before this book was published, God had already stated that creation was complete. "Thus the heavens and the earth were completed" (Genesis 2:1). The Bible agrees with this law of science because it is the Author of science who inspired the Bible.

4. The Second Law of Thermodynamics states that matter and energy become unusable, and thus, rather than evolving, the universe is actually running down—a fact also discovered in the early 1800s. Yet God had already stated thousands of years previously, "You, Lord, in

> ...From the **beginning**, from the **earliest times** of the earth...When He established the heavens, I was there, When He **inscribed a circle** on the face of the deep...
>
> - Proverbs 8:23, 27

the beginning laid the foundation of the earth, and the heavens are the works of Your hands; *they will perish*, but You remain; and *they all will become old* like a garment, and like a mantle You will roll them up; like a garment they will also be changed. But You are the same, and Your years will not come to an end" (Hebrews 1:10-12). It is logical that scripture would concur with the Second Law of Thermodynamics, because the Bible is inspired of God.

For the **life** of the flesh is in the **blood**...Its blood sustains its life.

- Leviticus 17:11, 14

5. Even in the time of George Washington, doctors were still practicing the treatment of "blood letting," that is, releasing blood from the body in an attempt to remove disease. If only science had paid more attention when God had warned, "Life is in the blood" (Leviticus 17:10-16), many lives would have been spared.

6. Thousands of years before science realized the value of sanitation and quarantine as a preventative measure against infectious diseases, God had given such instructions (Leviticus 13-14).

7. Man once thought the stars could be counted. In fact, Ptolemy, as late as 150 AD, listed only 3,000. Not until the invention of the telescope did man begin to realize the vastness of the universe. Yet all along, the Bible had described the number of the stars as innumerable, when the ancient prophet Jeremiah around 630 BC stated "the host of heaven cannot be numbered" (Jeremiah 33:22).

8. The water vapor cycle—that is, the process of rain, evaporation and condensation—is described in Job 36:27-28 when it states, "He draws up the drops of water, which distill as rain to the streams; the clouds pour down their moisture and abundant showers fall on mankind," yet Aristotle is thought to be the first to understand the production of rain through the water vapor cycle in 350 BC—some

two thousand years after it was described in scripture.

9. Man began to understand that both men and women have a seed of procreation in about 63 AD. Yet God had stated such thousands of years before in Genesis 3:15.

There are many more examples of the pre-scientific foreknowledge of the Bible. Check out Apologetics Press' resources online if you are interested in learning more.

Not only did the Bible state scientific principles long before they were discovered, how can one honestly account for the fact that the Bible does not contain *any* of the ignorance, superstition or junk science of the time in the surrounding cultures when it was written? None of the men who wrote the Bible claimed to be scientists, so how did they know all these things without having modern scientific tools or instruments? The Bible is beyond a doubt the words of our Creator.

Fulfilled Prophecy

The unlikely destruction of Tyre

The second line of evidence we will examine to prove the divine inspiration of the scriptures is that of fulfilled prophecy. A prophecy is a specific prediction of events yet to take place. In all of Greek and Latin literature, there is not one specific prophecy of a great historic event to come. And while other books such as the Koran or the Book of Mormon also claim to be from God, the Bible is the only book that contains a large body of prophecies relating to individual nations, cities, and peoples. These prophecies are not vague predictions or educated guesses. In fact, the Bible itself notes that in order to be considered a true prophet, one's predictions were to be 100 percent accurate concerning the future, 100 percent of the time (Deuteronomy 18:21-22). Certainly if the Bible truly contains the words of an infallible God who

...When a prophet speaks in the name of the Lord, **if the thing does not happen or come to pass**, that is the thing which the Lord has **not spoken**; the prophet has spoken it presumptuously; you shall not be afraid of him.

- Deuteronomy 18:22

> They will **destroy the walls of Tyre** and break down her towers; and I will **scrape her debris** from her and make her like a **bare rock**.
>
> - Ezekiel 26:4

knows all, including the future, we would expect the prophecies in the Bible to contain perfectly fulfilled prophecies.

The amazing thing to keep in mind is that the prophecies we will examine were physically recorded *long* before the events took place that fulfilled these prophecies.

One such example is the series of prophecies against the ancient city of Tyre, spoken between 595 and 570 BC (Ezekiel 1:2; 29:17). Ezekiel clearly predicted that God would make Tyre "a bare rock" (26:4), and even more specifically, "a place for the spreading of nets" (26:5); that its conquerors would "throw (its) stones, timbers and (its) debris into the water" (26:12), and that it would be "built no more" (26:14).

In 332 BC, over two hundred years after this prophecy was recorded, Alexander the Great warred against Tyre. In fear, the inhabitants deserted the mainland city to take up residence on the island city of Tyre a half mile offshore. Alexander built a causeway (which still exists today), connecting the mainland to the island city.

To build this land bridge, Alexander had the complete mainland city cast into the sea, even to the point of scraping off all the topsoil down to bedrock, as was predicted by God, Tyre became a bare rock. If one visits this site today, just as prophesied, one will find no mainland city but only a place fishermen still use to spread and dry their nets.

King Cyrus's name and dealings 150 years before his birth

Imagine you pick up a dusty, ancient book you know for a fact had been written in 1857. As you begin to read the book, the shocking reality sends shivers up your spine as you read your own name in it, along with the prediction of something monumental you had just accomplished. That is exactly what happened when God predicted, through the prophet Isaiah, more than 150 years in advance, the name of the specific individual who would serve His purpose of restoring Israel to her land (Isaiah 44:28). That man was Cyrus, founder of the Persian Empire, who first came to the throne of Anshan in Eastern Elam in 559 BC. In 549 he conquered the Medes and became the ruler of the combined Persian and Median Empire. In 539 he conquered Babylon (Daniel 5:30) and the very next year issued a decree that the Jews could return to Jerusalem and rebuild the temple (2 Chronicles 36:22-23; Ezra 1:1-4), thus fulfilling God's prophecy.

There are dozens of such prophecies that could also be explored, including:

- The fall of Babylon (Isaiah 13:19-22)

- The fall of Egypt (Isaiah 19; Ezekiel 29:30)

- The fall of Nineveh (Book of Nahum; Zephaniah 2:13-15, Isaiah 10:12-14)

- The fall of Sidon (Ezekiel 28:20-24)

The history and downfall of these once flourishing nations were predicted with minute details hundreds of years before the events took place. Only an all-knowing God could have known and inspired prophets to pen in scripture all these clear prophecies which have been fulfilled with such awesome precision (If you are interested in learning more about fulfilled Bible prophecies, read *The Bible on Trial* by Wayne Jackson).

Astonishingly accurate archeology

If the Bible were not inspired of God, archeology would unearth time and time again geographical and historic mistakes within it. Many archaeological discoveries confirm historical statements made in the Bible. Dozens of names of emperors, high priests, princes, and governors that are mentioned in the New Testament have been verified by archeology. There is no case where the Bible

> Who says of **Cyrus**, 'He is My shepherd, and he shall perform all My pleasure, saying to Jerusalem, "**You shall be built**," and to the temple, "**Your foundation shall be laid**."'
>
> - Isaiah 44:28

makes a geographical mistake. Although it lists 45 countries, each and every one is accurately placed and named, as are the 36 towns mentioned in the Bible. Without exception, when the Bible speaks, it is accurate. Archeology has unearthed amazing corroborative evidence that confirms the Bible's account of history as well. Archeology has proven that civilization originated in the Tigris Euphrates Valley, fossils on the top of mountains have confirmed the Great Flood, the famine in Egypt during Joseph's era, the walls of Jericho, Solomon's wealth, and many other Biblical truths. Each generation unearths more and more new evidence and is thus given fresh opportunities to acknowledge as true the Bible's claim to be the word of God. Without exception, when the Bible speaks, it is accurate.

The Bible's unity and harmony from one mind

What are the chances that you agree—even with your own spouse—on every topic? There is only one explanation why 40 very different human authors, living on three different continents, over a period of 1,500 years, penned the Bible, which covers thousands of topics, and yet there exists not even one contradiction in doctrinal teaching from Genesis to Revelation. Truly, there can be no other reason other than the fact that this miraculous harmony comes from one incomparable Mind— God's mind. It is because of the Bible's doctrinal unity that a preacher can cite passages from all over the Bible to make one point. The Bible is unified from beginning to end on topics that remain controversial even today. Every book of the Bible is essential; truly "The sum of Thy word is truth" (Psalm 119:160). Bert Thompson is spot on when he states, "It is as if the Bible were a magnificent symphony orchestrated by a single Conductor. The 'musicians' each may have played a different instrument, in a different place, at a different time. But when the talented Maestro combined the individual efforts, the end result was a striking

> The sum of Your word is **truth**, and every one of Your righteous ordinances is **everlasting**.
>
> - Psalm 119:160

masterpiece" (*In Defense of...the Bible's Inspiration [Part I]* by Bert Thompson, Ph.D.).

Sometimes you may hear someone state something like, "It's pretty obvious the Bible originally came from God, but how *can we trust the Bible we have today* to still be the original, authentic word of God? Has it been accurately preserved and translated over the centuries?"

Some have accused the early Catholics of removing portions of scripture. But be assured, the Old Testament was finished and was accepted as a complete collection centuries before the Catholic church ever existed. The books of the New Testament were accepted and known by Christians even before the first century closed and long before the arrival of the Catholic church (2 Peter 3:16). Our earliest New Testament manuscripts date all the way back to around 130 AD, and a complete New Testament manuscript exists which dates at 325 AD. When we compare the Bible manuscripts to other classical manuscripts, Bible accuracy is again confirmed. The fact that many modern versions such as "The Message" have been irresponsible—since the original Hebrew and Greek is at hand to compare the reliability of the translation—there is absolutely no proof that the original Bible has been corrupted over the centuries. Besides, logic tells us that certainly if God can create the entire universe, God is infinitely more powerful than any man or group of men, and as such, He obviously has the ability to keep His word accurate and available.

Jesus clearly said that His words would never pass away. "Heaven and earth will pass away, but My words will not pass away" (Matthew 24:35). And Peter said the word of the Lord is as dependable today as the day He spoke it. "...For you have been born again not of seed which is perishable but imperishable, that is, through the living and enduring word of God. For, 'All flesh is like grass, and all its glory like the flower of grass. The grass

Heaven and earth will pass away, but **My words will not pass away**.

- Matthew 24:35

withers, and the flower falls off, but the word of the Lord endures forever.' And this is the word which was preached to you" (1 Peter 1:23-25).

For generations, people have aggressively tried to eliminate the word of God. King Jehoiakim took his penknife, cut some of the words of the Old Testament Scriptures to pieces, and threw them into a fire (Jeremiah 36:22-23). During the Dark Ages, people tried to keep the Bible from the general population. In fact, those caught translating or distributing the Scriptures were sent to prison, tortured, and sometimes killed. The French skeptic Voltaire, centuries later, claimed "within fifty years, the Bible more than any other book will no longer be discussed among educated people." Yet the Bible still is being discussed all over the world, and few people today can even tell you who Voltaire was. Robert Ingersol, an American living in the early 1900s, stated regarding the Bible, "In fifteen years, I will have this book in the morgue." Needless to say, although Ingersol spent upon his death some time in a morgue, the Bible lives and abides as Jesus promised.

The Bible's understandability

Certainly if God can create the entire universe, God has the ability to communicate with those He created and loves. Surely if God is wise enough to keep the universe operating, He knows how to write a book that all honest men and women could understand alike. Why would God speak if not to be understood? If we cannot understand the Bible, then God has failed in His desire and His power is limited. On the contrary, God's word says itself that it *is* understandable (Ephesians 3:4); in fact we are divinely mandated to understand it (Ephesians 5:17). Be assured, if you earnestly seek to understand God's will, He promises you will find it. He also promises that He will reward those who diligently seek Him (Hebrews 11:6).

...when you read **you can understand** my insight into the mystery of Christ...

- Ephesians 3:4

To summarize, it makes sense God would want to communicate with His creation, and the Bible claims to be that communication. Undeniable evidence exists which proves this inspiration. There is evidence within fulfilled prophecies, which surpass the possibilities of any man to predict or foresee. There is evidence in the form of remarkably accurate archeology, its beautiful unity and harmony, and its astonishing pre-scientific foreknowledge. The Bible is accurate in every way: historically, geographically, and scientifically. It contains medical and scientific knowledge very much ahead of its time. Yet it does not include the medical and scientific ignorance found in the various eras in which it was written.

The Bible's dependability

The Bible truly came from God. Since we can trust the Bible when it comes to all things physical, it follows that we can count on the Bible to give us dependable answers to all our spiritual questions, including the ultimate question "What must I do to be prepared for eternity?"

2 Timothy 3:16-17 says, "All Scripture is inspired by God and profitable for teaching, for reproof, for correction, for training in righteousness; so that the man of God may be adequate, equipped for every good work," and 1 Peter 1:23-25 assures us "...for you have been born again not of seed which is perishable but imperishable, that is, through the living and enduring word of God. For, 'All flesh is like grass, and all its glory like the flower of grass. The grass withers, and the flower falls off, but the word of the Lord endures forever.' And this is the word which was preached to you."

Many people look for life's answers either by their feelings, their conscience, following the majority, or even putting all their trust in a religious leader, spiritual advisor, or someone they consider scholarly. It is *essential*, given what is at stake, that

So then do not be foolish, but **understand** what the will of the Lord is.

- Ephesians 5:17

all our religious beliefs come directly from God through His written word, the Bible:

a) In John 14:15, Jesus said "If you love Me, you will keep My commandments." Jesus wants us to express our love and appreciation for all He has done for us, by obeying Him. You could say obedience is God's "love language."

b) Yet God does not expect us to lead an ascetic lifestyle. 1 Corinthians 4:6 warns, "...learn not to exceed what is written, so that no one of you will become arrogant in behalf of one against the other." He wants us to enjoy both this life and especially the life to come.

> Do not **add** to His words or He will **reprove** you, and you will be proved a **liar**.
>
> - Proverbs 30:6

c) Proverbs 30:6 warns us, "Do not add to His words." It's comforting to know that we need not create additional rules or expectations in order to please God.

In fact, note from the following passages how important it is not to replace God's teachings with teachings originating with mere men.

d) Galatians 1:8-9 cautions, "But even if we, or an angel from heaven, should preach to you a gospel contrary to what we have preached to you, he is to be accursed! As we have said before, so I say again now, if any man is preaching to you a gospel contrary to what you received, he is to be accursed!" Paul makes this statement twice for emphasis. It is imperative that we only preach the original gospel taught accurately by the apostles. We must be able to cite a Bible book, chapter and verse for all religious beliefs we hold in our hearts and preach from our pulpits.

e) 1 Timothy 6:3-5 says, "If anyone advocates a different doctrine and does not agree with sound words, those of our Lord Jesus Christ, and with the doctrine conforming to godliness, he is conceited and understands nothing; but he has a morbid interest in controversial questions and disputes about words, out of which arise envy, strife, abusive language, evil suspicions, and constant friction between men of depraved mind and deprived of the truth, who suppose that godliness is a means of gain." If we want to be considered humble by God and have integrity as His servant, we must only advocate the doctrines (that is, teachings) of the Lord.

f) Again, 2 John 9 warns, "Anyone who goes too far and does not abide in the teaching of Christ, does not have God; the one who abides in the teaching, he has both the Father and the Son." Let's make sure all that we believe and teach come directly from the Bible.

The Scriptures address every deep need of man. It answers every fundamental question we have, such as, "Where did life originate?" "How did the universe begin?" "Why are we here?" "What happens after death?" "How will the world end?" "How do I prepare to meet my God?" The scriptures answer all these questions and more, fulfilling our spiritual, social, psychological, and emotional needs.

The Bible gives us clear and livable guidelines of how to both please our Creator and live a more joy-filled life. What an amazing truth and blessing that we can bring joy to our heavenly Father and experience great joy ourselves in the process!

Jesus Christ: Your Savior

In this series of lessons we have discussed the unquestionable fact that there is a God—the creation is just too complex and wonderful to have any other logical explanation other than that it is the product of the ultimate Engineer, Designer, and Artist.

In lesson two we carefully examined the Bible and found that it must, too, be only the result of an omniscient Author and no less than God's revelation to man, His revealed will for mankind. The Scriptures are His own explanation, word for word, of who He is and how He wants us to relate to Him.

In this lesson we will address the fundamental message of the Bible, the primary reason for God speaking to us, and it is because we have all sinned and are due eternal death for those sins. But Jesus Christ, the Son of God, took the punishment due us when He allowed Himself to be crucified. The fundamental message of the Bible is that our eternal destiny depends upon our response to this truth.

Before we examine the evidence that confirms the proposition that Jesus is the Son of God, first let's hear from the mouth of Jesus Himself who He claimed to be. In Matthew 16:16, Jesus praises and blesses Peter's explanation of who Jesus is when Peter says, "You are the Christ, the Son of the living God." When Peter acknowledged Jesus as "the Christ," the word he used, in Hebrew, means "Messiah," indicating that Jesus Christ is the Savior, Priest, and King prophesied about and eagerly anticipated throughout the ancient Old Testament writings.

Simon Peter answered, "**You are the Christ, the Son of the living God.**" And Jesus said to him, "Blessed are you, Simon Barjona, because flesh and blood did not reveal this to you, but **My Father who is in heaven**.

- Matthew 16:16-17

We need not, however, rest our faith upon the testimony of Peter alone. Angels declared to Mary the mother of Jesus, "...the holy Child shall be called the Son of God" (Luke 1:35). The truth of Jesus' divine position as the only begotten Son of God was declared publicly and audibly in heaven by the Father Himself upon the baptism of Jesus. "After being baptized, Jesus came up immediately from the water; and behold, the heavens were opened, and he saw the Spirit of God descending as a dove and lighting on Him, and behold, a voice out of the heavens said, 'This is My beloved Son, in whom I am well-pleased'" (Matthew 3:16-17).

Is Jesus who He claimed to be? Were Peter and the angels correct when they called Jesus the Christ and Son of God? History tells us, and everyone admits, Jesus existed as a first century Jew, a religious teacher, who lived in Palestine. You may hear someone argue that Jesus was a good man with good moral teachings but no more than a man and certainly not a Savior. Yet, logically, there can be only two alternatives: Jesus is either the Son of God as He claimed, the anticipated Messiah and Savior of mankind, or He was a manipulative liar and imposter filled with selfish ambition. The reason why He cannot be merely a good man is because a good man does not say He is equal with God (John 5:17-18). A good man does not claim He deserves the degree of respect which is only reserved for God (John 5:23) or that if one does not obey Him, he is not obeying God (5:23). He claimed that He would judge mankind (5:22, 27). He claimed the ability and power to forgive sin (Mark 2:10). He claimed His words would outlast the creation itself (Matthew 24:35). He claimed an eternal pre-existence (John 8:58). Immediately these statements force us to make a choice. Jesus is either God in the flesh or a liar. There is no middle ground.

The most convicting evidence that Jesus is who He says is the astounding number of predictions that

> For this reason therefore the Jews were seeking all the more to kill Him, because He...was calling God **His own Father**, making Himself **equal with God**.
>
> - John 5:18

were written about Him 400-1,000 years before they occurred. The Old Testament contains over 450 messianic prophecies. Every one of these prophecies was fulfilled with 100% accuracy. The skeptic may ask, "Couldn't someone just write these down and pretend they were written earlier?" The discovery of the Dead Sea Scrolls put to rest most of such arguments. What are the Dead Sea Scrolls? They are 900 documents, including texts from the Hebrew Bible, that were discovered between 1956 and 1979 in 11 caves in and around the Wadi Qumran in the West Bank. According to carbon dating, textual analysis, and handwriting analysis, the documents were written at various times between the middle of the 2nd century BC and the 1st century AD, and The Great Isaiah Scroll has been carbon dated to a range of 335 BC—107 BC. Since this discovery, no one can deny these predictions existed hundreds of years before their fulfillment. We know that David, the author of Psalm 22, lived from about 1043 to 973 BC. Psalm 22 is especially amazing since it predicted 11 events surrounding Jesus' crucifixion about a thousand years before they happened.

Another skeptic may ask, "Couldn't any imposter make it their mission in life to try to fulfill prophecies in order to appear to be the Messiah?" Yet note as we go through these prophecies how many of them are not under human control. In other words, if someone tried to fulfill all of them, how could they arrange to be born in Bethlehem or that the price for one's betrayal would be exactly 30 pieces of silver? Most of the occurrences on the chart we are about to examine could not be fulfilled by one's own efforts but instead were actions happening around and to Jesus. Here are just a few dozen of the hundreds of fulfilled prophecies predicted regarding the life of Jesus, your Savior:

Psalm 22 is especially amazing since it **predicted 11 events** surrounding Jesus' crucifixion about **a thousand years** before they happened.

Old Testament Scriptures That Predict Events in the Life of the Coming Messiah		
The Messianic prophecy	**Where the prophecy appears in the Old Testament (written between 1450 BC and 430 BC)**	**Jesus' fulfillment of the prophecy in the New Testament (written between 45 and 95 AD)**
The Messiah would be a descendant of Abraham	Genesis 12:3; 18:18	Acts 3:25, 26
The Messiah would be a descendant of Judah	Genesis 49:10	Matthew 1:2; Luke 3:33
The Messiah would be raised from the dead (resurrected)	Psalm 16:10, 11	Matthew 28:5-9; Mark 16:6; Luke 24:4-7; John 20:11-16; Acts 1:3; 2:32
The Messiah would be crucified	Psalm 22 (contains 11 prophecies—not all listed here)	Matthew 27:34-50; John 19:17-30
The Messiah would be sneered at and mocked	Psalm 22:7	Luke 23:11, 35-39
The Messiah's feet and hands would be pierced.	Psalm 22:16	Luke 23:33; 24:36-39; John 19:18; 20:19-20, 24-27
The Messiah's bones would not be broken (although a person's legs were usually broken after being crucified)	Psalm 22:17; 34:20	John 19:31-33, 36
Men would gamble for the Messiah's clothing	Psalm 22:18	Matthew 27:35; Mark 15:24; Luke 23:34; John 19:23, 24
The Messiah would be accused by false witnesses	Psalm 35:11	Matthew 26:59, 60; Mark 14:56, 57
The Messiah would be betrayed by a friend	Psalm 41:9	John 13:18, 21
The Messiah would ascend to heaven (at the right hand of God)	Psalm 68:18	Luke 24:51; Acts 1:9
The Messiah would be given vinegar and gall to drink	Psalm 69:21	Matthew 27:34; Mark 15:23; John 19:29, 30
The Messiah would be a descendant of David	Psalm 132:11; Jeremiah 23:5, 6; 33:15, 16	Luke 1:32, 33
The Messiah would be born of a virgin	Isaiah 7:14	Matthew 1:18-25; Luke 1:26-35

The Messiah's first ministry would be in Galilee	Isaiah 9:1-7	Matthew 4:12-16
The Messiah would heal, make the blind to see, the deaf to hear...	Isaiah 35:5-6	Matthew 11:3-6; John 11:47
The Messiah would be beaten, mocked, and spat upon	Isaiah 50:6	Matthew 26:67; 27:26-31
People would hear yet not believe the "arm of the LORD" (Messiah)	Isaiah 53:1	John 12:37, 38
The Messiah would be rejected	Isaiah 53:3	Matthew 27:20-25; Mark 15:8-14; Luke 23:18-23; John 19:14, 15
The Messiah would be killed	Isaiah 53:5-9	Matthew 27:50; Mark 15:37-39
The Messiah would be silent in front of his accusers	Isaiah 53:7	Matthew 26:62, 63; 27:12-14
The Messiah would be buried with the rich	Isaiah 53:9	Matthew 27:59, 60; Mark 15:46; Luke 23:52, 53; John 19:38-42
The Messiah would be crucified with criminals	Isaiah 53:12	Matthew 27:38; Mark 15:27; Luke 23:32, 33
The Messiah would establish a new and everlasting covenant	Isaiah 55:3-4; Jeremiah 31:31-34	Matthew 26:28; Mark 14:24; Luke 22:20; Hebrews 8:6-13
The Messiah would be our intercessor	Isaiah 59:16	Hebrews 9:15
The Messiah would come during the Roman Empire	Daniel 2:36-45	Luke 2:1
The Messiah would be born in Bethlehem	Micah 5:2	Matthew 2:1; Luke 2:4-7
The Messiah would enter Jerusalem riding a donkey	Zechariah 9:9	Matthew 21:1-11
The Messiah would be sold for 30 pieces of silver	Zechariah 11:12, 13	Matthew 26:15; Matthew 27:3-10
The Messiah would be forsaken by His disciples	Zechariah 13:7	Matthew 26:31, 56

(Adapted from http://www.clarifyingchristianity.com/m_prophecies.shtml)

Professor Emeritus of Science at Westmont College, Peter Stoner, has calculated the probability of one man fulfilling the major prophecies made concerning the Messiah. His mathematicians have calculated the probability of just 48 predictions being accidentally fulfilled in one man. The probability came out to be just 1 in 10 to the 157th power. That is one in ten followed by 157 zeros. If that is the improbability of 48 predictions being fulfilled by coincidence, what would that number be if all 456 predictions were fulfilled?

Jesus truly is the predicted Messiah and Savior of mankind. Fulfilled prophecy proves it. His miracles prove it. His resurrection proves it. It makes sense then that Jesus would be completely devoid of worldly ambition and in fact would refuse to become king when others tried to make Him so (John 6:15), for He already has all power. It makes sense that He spoke confidently as one who possessed all truth, that He was entirely free of prejudices or fear. It makes sense that He accepted worship (John 9:35-38, Matthew 28:9) for He is our Holy God in the flesh. No wonder He gave the greatest moral standard the world has ever known. As you get to know your Savior through Holy Scripture, He is described in many ways and wears many titles. Each one gives us a clearer picture of who He is and what He does. Jesus is called our **Advocate** (1 John 2:1) because He strongly supports us. Because of His power, He is called the **Almighty** (Reveleation 1:8; Matthew 28:18). Jesus is called the **Bread of Life** (John 6:35; 6:48) because He sustains us spiritually. Our Lord is called the **Bridegroom** (Matthew 9:15) because of His intimate relationship with the church, and the **Good Shepherd** (John 10:11, 14) for His tender care over each of our souls. He is the **Creator** (John 1:3) and the **Deliverer** (Romans 11:26) who rescues us from sin. He refers to Himself as the **Gate** (John 10:9) because it is through Him that we enter our home in heaven. Jesus is our **High Priest** (Hebrews 2:17) for He makes intercession

And behold, Jesus met them and greeted them. And they came up and took hold of His feet and **worshiped Him**.

- Matthew 28:9

for us to the Father. He is our **Hope** (1 Timothy 1:1), for without His sacrifice we could not live in expectation of a heavenly reward. When Jesus was called the **Lamb of God** (John 1:29) it represented His being sacrificed for the forgiveness of our sins. He is called the **Light of the World** (John 8:12) because He gives us clear direction, lighting our way. Jesus is our **Rock** (1 Corinthians 10:4) for He brings to us stability and protection. John describes Jesus as the **True Vine** (John 15:1) because it is He who makes our lives truly fruitful and productive; finally, He is called the **Way** (John 14:6) because there is no other way to heaven except through Jesus Christ. Jesus is undeniably the **Son of God**, and during His ministry He taught the world's most invaluable truths, including the most important question in your life and mine—that being, "What must I do to prepare to meet God and experience a joyful eternity?"

Jesus said in Mark 16:16, "He who has believed and has been baptized shall be saved; but he who has disbelieved shall be condemned."

After Jesus was crucified, buried, resurrected, and returned to heaven, Jesus' apostles faithfully carried out this same message of salvation. Listen to how the first recorded sermon is consistent with what Jesus taught we need to do to prepare for eternity. Peter speaks here to the very people who had crucified Jesus. "'Therefore let all the house of Israel know for certain that God has made Him both Lord and Christ—this Jesus whom you crucified.' Now when they heard this, they were pierced to the heart, and said to Peter and the rest of the apostles, 'Brethren, what shall we do?' Peter said to them, 'Repent, and let each of you be baptized in the name of Jesus Christ for the forgiveness of your sins; and you will receive the gift of the Holy Spirit. For the promise is for you and your children and for all who are far off, as many as the Lord our God will call to Himself.' And with many other words he solemnly testified and kept on exhorting them,

> Jesus said to him, "**I am the way**, and the truth, and the life; no one comes to the Father but **through Me**.
>
> - John 14:6

saying, 'Be saved from this perverse generation!' So then, those who had received his word were baptized; and that day there were added about three thousand souls" (Acts 2:36-41).

Belief in Jesus as the Son of God and Savior of mankind, and baptism in order to receive the forgiveness of our sins and to be saved from eternal condemnation, is consistent with what Jesus said we all need to do in order to seek God, and it is consistent with what all the apostles taught in the early church. Of course, in order to learn everything that is involved in our salvation, we must study scripture as a whole, for obviously not every verse that speaks about salvation includes everything that God says saves us. For example:

a) Romans 10:10 says, "...with the heart a person believes, resulting in righteousness, and with the mouth he confesses, resulting in salvation" (only belief and confession are mentioned in this verse).

b) 1 Peter 3:21 says, "baptism now saves you—not the removal of dirt from the flesh, but an appeal to God for a good conscience—through the resurrection of Jesus Christ" (only baptism is mentioned in this verse).

c) Acts 11:18: "...God has granted to the Gentiles also the repentance that leads to life" (only repentance is mentioned).

d) Ephesians 2:8: "For by grace you have been saved through faith; and that not of yourselves, it is the gift of God" (only grace and faith are here mentioned).

> The process of preparing for heaven is the same for everyone: **faith**, **repentance**, **confession**, **baptism**, and **living a life that honors God**.

The process of preparing for heaven is the same for everyone: *faith* in God and His plan to save us, *repentance* (that is, discontinuing sinful habits), *confession* or admittance that Jesus is God's Son and your Savior, and *baptism* (which is immersion in water, a symbol of rebirth for the forgiveness of sins), and *living a life that honors God*. This process never varies. Note though, that no *one* verse in scripture has all elements God has chosen to save us. God expects us to be attentive enough to His word to search the scriptures, learn how to receive salvation and live a God-honoring life.

Having already noted the wonderful response in Acts 2 of those who had crucified Jesus yet still responded to Peter's sermon, choosing salvation and the resulting restoration to a close relationship with God, let's look at another person's enthusiastic response to hearing about the life of Jesus. "Then Philip opened his mouth, and beginning from this Scripture he preached Jesus to him. As they went along the road they came to some water; and the eunuch said, 'Look! Water! What prevents me from being baptized?' [And Philip said, *'If you believe with all your heart, you may.'* And he answered and said, *'I believe that Jesus Christ is the Son of God.'*] And he ordered the chariot to stop; and they both *went down into the water*, Philip as well as the eunuch, and he baptized him. When they *came up out of the water*, the Spirit of the Lord snatched Philip away; and the eunuch no longer saw him, but went on his way rejoicing" (Acts 8:35-39).

We learn in this case that—rather than sprinkling or pouring of water—immersion in water is the Biblical mode of baptism. This is consistent with the very Greek definition of the word "baptism." Also note that Philip said one must believe with all one's heart in order to qualify for baptism. Logic follows then that we need not concern ourselves with baptizing our babies, since an infant cannot believe nor has the infant any sin needing to be removed.

The last example we will explore is the conversion of the apostle Paul. In this case, Paul turns from being a persecutor of the church to being a vital member of the very church he once tried to destroy. "Now Saul, still breathing threats and murder against the disciples of the Lord, went to the high priest, and asked for letters from him to the synagogues at Damascus, so that if he

Now why do you delay? Get up and **be baptized**, and wash away your sins, calling on His name.

- Acts 22:16

found any belonging to the Way, both men and women, he might bring them bound to Jerusalem. As he was traveling, it happened that he was approaching Damascus, and suddenly a light from heaven flashed around him; and he fell to the ground and heard a voice saying to him, 'Saul, Saul, why are you persecuting Me?' And he said, 'Who are You, Lord?' And He said, 'I am Jesus whom you are persecuting, but get up and enter the city, and it will be told you what you must do.' The men who traveled with him stood speechless, hearing the voice but seeing no one. Saul got up from the ground, and though his eyes were open, he could see nothing; and leading him by the hand, they brought him into Damascus. And he was three days without sight, and neither ate nor drank" (Acts 9:1-9). Later in the book of Acts, Paul recounts what Ananias had told him to do three days after Paul had repented and believed: "Now why do you delay? Get up and be baptized, and wash away your sins, calling on His name" (Acts 22:16).

In the story of Paul's conversion, it is important to note that although Saul (later called Paul) had believed for three days, he still had sins to be washed away through baptism. The firm belief or faith Paul had experienced three days earlier did not remove Saul's sins, for he had not yet been baptized or born again. He was told by the messenger Ananias that he still had sins to be "washed away" through baptism. Obviously, forgiveness and the removal of sin follow baptism.

We, like the apostle Paul, have all sinned and are due eternal death for those sins. Yet Jesus Christ, the Son of God, generously took the punishment due us when He allowed Himself to be crucified. Our prayer for you today is that you will, in appreciation for His sacrifice, choose to believe the evidence that Jesus truly is the Son of God and your Savior, that you will repent of the sins that have held you in cruel bondage for so long, that you will confess your conviction that Jesus Christ is the Son of God, and that you will be baptized, reborn to start a new life in service to your Lord. This is when your fresh start begins.

A wonderful thing follows baptism, and that is being added by God to His family, the church. Jesus knew we would need one another for support in a world that is beautiful and joy-filled, yet is often distressing. In our next lesson, we will explore this wonderful relationship with Christ and His church and the many blessings to be enjoyed by being a part of His church.

The Church, God's Family

Imagine Christianity minus the circus, hypocrisy and complex power structures of denominations. Imagine Christianity minus every man-made rule and human tradition imposed these last 2,000 years of church history. That's the original, simple, pre-denominational (even pre-Catholic) Christianity this lesson addresses. God could have opted for a sort of "isolated Christianity" found alone in the woods—and while such would have certainly helped, prevented and resolved many personal problems and helped one face mortality with confidence—God in His perfect wisdom knew we would need more. Much more. God knew we would need faith-filled people to be alongside us as we watch a loved one die, or a safety net of love when we lose a job, or support from intelligent believers to help us think through and apply God's written wisdom to complex problems, and He knew we would need friends who are like family to celebrate the good times like graduations, a new baby, the marriage of our children and all the other milestones that feel more joyous when shared. He created us to thrive in community with one another.

> ...I will build **My church**; and the gates of Hades will not overpower it.
>
> - Matthew 16:18

God knew that in order to get over ourselves, we would need to learn to get along with a lot of people. These people may have a huge range of baggage, but we learn to love, help, and pray for them, likewise, they for us. God knew that you and I wouldn't even have a deep sense of purpose until we expended either blood, sweat, or tears learning to be "others-centered" in the most relevant cause on the planet: Christ. God knew we were going to need people in our life to help lift us out of the pit of sin from time to time, and they you. Also, God

...not forsaking our own **assembling together**, as is the habit of some, but **encouraging one another**; and all the more as you see the day drawing near.

- Hebrews 10:25

knew we needed a purpose, and our purpose is this: to bring Him glory. Consider this:

Is there anything valuable enough to you that you'd be willing to purchase it if the only currency accepted was the blood of your child? Unthinkable! And yet God says that the life of His Son is the price He willingly paid to "purchase the church," the very church with which He says we must not "forsake assembling" (Hebrews 10:25). If the church, which God passionately calls His "bride" (2 Corinthians 11:2), is so valuable to God He'd purchase it with His blood, I too must treasure what He treasures. This truth alone ends the egocentric question, "Can I have a meaningful relationship with God without the drama of committing to God's people, the church?" To even venture such a question is a supreme insult to the Bride of Christ. When we understand that, it becomes crystal clear that there's much more to consider about *how* to draw near to God than what we find easiest, or our personal preferences, or what feels good. Would I rather be close to God by taking a Sunday hike in the sunshine than gathering with believers? The truth is, it's not about me. It's not even about you. Life is about honoring His holiness and loving Him according to *His* "love language," not our own.

In the previous lesson, we considered evidence proving Jesus is who He claimed to be. We discovered His plan for saving us and how each of us can respond to His plan by having an intelligent faith, based upon real evidence that there is a God. We looked at objective proof that the Bible is God's word, that Jesus is the Savior He says He is, and that upon discontinuing a lifestyle of sin and obeying Jesus' command to be baptized as a symbol of our rebirth and Jesus' death, burial, and resurrection, we can begin a relationship with Him. Jesus is everything we need. He created us and loves us as we love the children we ourselves have brought into the world. His ultimate goal is similar to the desire we have for our own children—that is, our children's genuine happiness and well-being.

The church, God's family, is intended to be one of God's sources of happiness and productivity for all Christians, and that is what we will be considering in this lesson.

From the very beginning of creation, God stated, "It is not good for man to be alone." The initial solution to this problem of "aloneness" was the creation of woman who could be both man's companion and his helper. Yet another source of companionship in the worship of God is the church, or family of God. This is why God established the church—for the support and happiness of the children He loves and through this love to be glorified.

Throughout the ancient writings of the Old Testament, prophets (or spokesmen for God) predicted God's plan for mankind's needs and His own glory by establishing a church, or what sometimes is also called "The Kingdom" (Revelation 1:5-6) or "The body of Christ" (Ephesians 1:22). These prophecies were very specific as to who would be the founder of this church, when this church would be established, and where it would begin. Any organization founded by someone other than Christ, at a different time in history than Biblically predicted, or from a different location than scripture has identified, would be a man-made, extra-Biblical organization—not the simple, pristine kingdom predicted in scripture. The remainder of this lesson is rather meaty for readers less accustomed to Biblical studies. I welcome you to buckle up and zone in for the next couple pages.

Let's consider first, **who would establish the church?** In 2 Samuel 7:12, King David, who lived 1,000 years before Christ, was told that one of his descendants would "...establish the throne of His kingdom forever." Jesus Christ is that descendant of David. This explains why God chose to begin the New Testament with the genealogy that proves Jesus' relationship to King David. By showing that Jesus, through Mary, was a descendant of King David, an important piece of evidence was brought

This is why God established the church— for the **support and happiness** of the children He loves and through this love to be **glorified**.

forth proving He is the Messiah, the one who would establish a heavenly kingdom, the church. In fact, when Mary's part in God's plan was revealed, she is told regarding the Son she would bear, that, "... the Lord God will give Him the throne of His father David; and He will reign over the house of Jacob forever, and His kingdom will have no end" (Luke 1:32-33). We learn from these prophecies that Jesus and Jesus alone would be the establisher of this spiritual kingdom, or church.

The second question we want to consider is, **when would this kingdom, or church, be established?** A very short time before the establishment of the kingdom, both Jesus and John the baptizer preached, "The time is fulfilled, and the kingdom of God is at hand; repent and believe in the gospel" (Mark 1:15). The time that had been predicted for the coming of the kingdom had been fulfilled. In the first century, when Jesus and John preached the kingdom as being "at hand" this indicated it was right around the corner, or as we'd say, "close enough to touch." So close was the birth of the church that Jesus promised to some who were listening to Him preach that, "Truly I say to you, there are some of those who are standing here who shall not taste death until they see the kingdom of God after it has come with power" (Mark 9:1).

The New Testament reveals that the kingdom of God, the church, was established in the first century, during the days of the Roman emperors (Matthew 3:1; Luke 3:1-3; Mark 9:1; Acts 2:47; Colossians 1:12-14). It's no coincidence that God's prophet Daniel placed the establishment of the kingdom of God within the lifetime of Roman Empire (Daniel 2:40-43). Indeed that is what happened about 500 years later; during the days of the Roman Caesars, the kingdom of God was established. Christ lived and died while Rome ruled, just as Daniel had predicted. Obviously Rome no longer rules the world and hasn't for 1,000 years,

Now in the fifteenth year of the reign of **Tiberius Caesar**... the **word of God came to John**, the son of Zacharias, in the wilderness.

- Luke 3:1-2

yet the prophecy stated that the kingdom of God would arrive while the fourth empire was still ruling and still intact. Just as Daniel's vision predicted, today Rome is no longer a dominant kingdom, yet two thousand years later, the church, God's kingdom, still exists and always will.

During His ministry, Jesus Himself stated plainly, "I will build My church" (Matthew 16:18). There is no reasonable alternative but to believe that the kingdom Jesus announced as "at hand" was the spiritual Davidic kingdom promised to King David and the throne of David that the angel had promised to Mary (Luke 1:32).

Remember, Jesus said the kingdom of God would come with power. "Truly I say to you, there are some of those who are standing here who shall not taste death until they see the kingdom of God after it has come *with power*" (Mark 9:1). Power was again mentioned when Jesus, right before His ascension back into heaven, told his apostles, "I am sending forth the promise of My Father upon you; but you are to stay in the city until you are clothed *with power* from on high." In Acts 1:3 as Jesus was "...speaking of the things concerning the kingdom of God," He further explained, "...you will *receive power* when the Holy Spirit has come upon you; and you shall be My witnesses both in Jerusalem, and in all Judea and Samaria, and even to the remotest part of the earth" (Acts 1:8). Such power came upon the apostles the day the church was born, on the day of Pentecost. This was a wonderful day for God to plan its arrival, for it was a feast day when thousands of people had gathered who would unexpectedly witness such an amazing display of God's power and would hear from God's inspired apostles God's plan for saving them through Christ. In fact, upon the apostle Peter's first address to the crowd, you may remember the response from these grateful people was, "when they heard this, they were pierced to the heart, and said to Peter and the rest of the apostles, 'Brethren, what shall

...I am sending forth the **promise of My Father** upon you; but you are to stay in the city until you are clothed **with power** from on high.

- Luke 24:49

we do?' Peter said to them, 'Repent, and each of you be baptized in the name of Jesus Christ for the forgiveness of your sins; and you will receive the gift of the Holy Spirit. For the promise is for you and your children and for all who are far off, as many as the Lord our God will call to Himself.' And with many other words he solemnly testified and kept on exhorting them, saying, 'Be saved from this perverse generation!' So then, those who had received his word were baptized; and that day there were added about three thousand souls" (Acts 2:37-41).

We know the church Jesus established came into existence on this day, because following this event, every time the Bible addresses the topic of the church or kingdom of God, it speaks of it in the present tense, as being in existence. Christians in the first century were said to have received a kingdom that cannot be shaken (Hebrews 12:28) and Christians in the first century were said to have been added to God's kingdom (Colossians 1:13).

> Therefore, since we receive a **kingdom** which cannot be shaken...
>
> - Hebrews 12:28

We've discovered so far in this lesson *why* the Lord established the church, *who* would establish it, and *when*. But where would the church begin? The church started in Jerusalem, which was predicted as the point of origin for "God's house" in Isaiah 2, and just as that prophecy predicted, a law went forth from Jerusalem, and that law was the "law of liberty" or gospel of Christ. It was the beginning of a new Covenant, not with only one nation, the nation of Israel, but a Covenant (that is, a solemn agreement) with *all* from *any* nation that wanted to have a relationship with God. They could now be "spiritual descendants of Abraham"—anyone could become a child of God. Regardless of race, anyone could become a part of this new spiritual Israel.

It has been almost 2,000 years since the birthday of the church, and a lot has happened since. One thing has *not* happened, though (as we have already addressed in this lesson): the church established by Jesus Christ has not become extinct. Remember, God has promised through the prophet Daniel that this kingdom would "never be destroyed." Thousands of churches have come into existence since the first century. And sadly, many of them have lost trust in God's written word. Too often, churches take little time or effort to listen to or heed carefully the written word of God, even on subjects as critical and basic as what one must do to prepare for eternity.

How To Find or Restore New Testament Christianity

So how do I find a church to worship with that honors and obeys the word of God, like the faithful church in the Bible? The church in the New Testament had distinguishing characteristics that still help us identify it. Any group today can return to God's pattern and restore New Testament Christianity.

- Jesus established His church. In Matthew 16:18 Jesus stated, "I will build My church; and the gates of Hades will not overpower it." Incidentally, note that the word "church" is singular. Jesus built one church. This is in harmony with Ephesians 4:4 where God's word says, "There is one body," and Ephesians 1:22-23 defining His body as being the church. There are many congregations of believers, but there should only be one doctrinally unified church universally.

Another distinguishing characteristic of the original church is that...

- Jesus is the exclusive head of His church. Ephesians 1:22-23 says, "He put all things in subjection under His feet, and gave Him as head over all things to the church, which is His body, the fullness of Him who fills all in all." Since Christ is the head over all things to the church, I don't have to concern myself with keeping the rules created by level after level of complicated

There is **one body** and one Spirit, just as also you were called in one hope of your calling...

- Ephesians 4:4

church hierarchy, nor must I fund all this non-Biblical machinery, mega-church buildings and unnecessary church government.

The next distinguishing characteristic of the church is the same basic thing that distinguishes individuals from one another.

- His church wears His name. There are a number of different names for the church in the Bible, including "church of Christ" mentioned in Romans 16:16 when it says, "All the churches of Christ salute you." "Church of God" or "church of the Firstborn" are other scriptural examples. Finding a church that wears a name found in scripture is one indication that a church mindfully honors God and His word.

- Individual members of His church wear His name. 1 Peter 4:16 says, "...but if a man suffer as a Christian, let him not feel ashamed; but let him glorify God in this name." Just as when a wife takes on a husband's name it is an honor to him, similarly, when Christ's people wear His name, "Christian," rather than a man-made name, it glorifies Christ.

- His church worships scripturally—that is, "in spirit and in truth" (John 4:24) on the first day of the week (Acts 20:7). Many in our culture have a very casual view of worship and assume that God accepts anything they feel like doing as worship. Yet the truth that the Bible repeatedly reveals is that even from the first recorded time worship was offered to God, Abel's worship was acceptable, but not his brother Cain's (Genesis 4). So, worshipping God has never been "anywhere your heart takes you." In fact, the first day of temple worship for the nation of Israel, two priests "did their own thing" instead of following God's instructions regarding how He wanted to be worshiped, and they lost their lives—the invaluable lesson being: worshipping our holy God His way is serious business. King

On the **first day of the week**, when we were **gathered together** to break bread...

- Acts 20:7

Saul lost his entire kingdom when he offered to God sacrifices that God did not authorize (1 Samuel 15). Any serious student of the Bible quickly learns from these examples that we must not honor God in any manner we want or personally find entertaining. God wants to be honored in the ways He has specified He wants to be honored. Obedient adoration is God's love language. God is holy, and it is imperative that we honor Him as such. For century after century, all Christians understood this and worshipped in the same, simple, Biblical manner:

1) Participating in the **Lord's Supper**—that is, remembering Christ's death, burial, and resurrection by partaking weekly with other Christians of unleavened bread, symbolic of the precious sacrifice of Christ's body on the cross for our sins, and the fruit of the vine, symbolizing His blood which removed our sins and established His new covenant.

2) **Praying**, which includes not only expressing our needs and the needs of others to God but also confession of sin, expressions of gratitude for what He has already provided, and praise for all our Lord is and all He does (Acts 2:42).

3) **Gathering of a free will offering** was also a practice of the early church. While this is often overemphasized in many denominations with mega budgets, it is something necessary to continue the work of getting the gospel into the world and caring for those truly in need within the church (1 Corinthians 16:1-2).

4) Listening to **teaching** based upon scripture was also an important aspect of the worship of the early church and is still an important way of learning how to please God and make the most of one's life (Acts 2:42).

5) For centuries, **singing** was always a simple and beautiful expression of one's heartfelt

> They were continually **devoting** themselves to the apostles' **teaching** and to **fellowship**, to the **breaking of bread** and to **prayer**.
>
> - Acts 2:42

...speaking to one another in psalms and hymns and spiritual songs, **singing** and **making melody with your heart** to the Lord...

- Ephesians 5:19

love and devotion for God. In early church history, God did not "share the spotlight" or divide the glory and praise with any performing soloist or rock band but, during public worship, received all the glory Himself. Beginning slowly about 600 years after the church was established, musical instruments were gradually added without God's authorization until today the focus has evolved into entertainment-focused performances, an entire substitution of our human preferences for the divine pattern for church worship (Ephesians 5:19).

Another distinguishing characteristic of the original church is that...

- A Biblical church preaches God's complete salvation plan. Jesus' instructions to His disciples was that they were to "Go therefore and make disciples of all the nations, baptizing them in the name of the Father and the Son and the Holy Spirit, teaching them to observe all that I commanded you" (Matthew 28:19-20).

He clearly states in Mark 16:16, "He who has believed and has been baptized shall be saved; but he who has disbelieved shall be condemned." The apostle Peter in the third chapter of his epistle uses the worldwide flood of Noah's era to explain that the baptism through which God has chosen to save us is water baptism. "God kept waiting in the days of Noah, during the construction of the ark, in which a few, that is, eight persons, were brought safely through the water. Corresponding to that, *baptism now saves you*—not the removal of dirt from the flesh, but an appeal to God for a good conscience—through the resurrection of Jesus Christ" (1 Peter 3:20-12). Has there ever been a more overwhelming visual aid for water baptism than the flood of Noah?

Note that many denominations today teach salvation by faith alone, yet the *only* time the Bible mentions "faith alone" is when it says in James 2:24, "You see that a man is justified by works and *not by faith alone.*" There are many things that the Bible says are involved in our salvation: God's grace, the blood of Christ, but never one thing alone.

There are more distinguishing characteristics of the church.

- Biblical church organization

    1) A church that seeks to be scriptural will organize itself in the simple manner in which the original church was organized. Biblical church organization includes **elders**, the same office called at other times in scriptures "bishops," "overseers," "pastors," "presbyters," "rulers," or "shepherds." These men have to meet certain qualifications specified by God (Titus 1:5-9). For example, one of the qualifications to hold the office of elder is that an elder must be a married man with believing children. Obviously then, to call an unmarried teenager an "elder" (as the Mormon church does) does not honor but in fact disregards the authority of God's word.

    2) The church also has **deacons**. These are servants and helpers who are under the oversight of elders. Note in 1 Timothy 3:12 that a deacon, like an elder, is required by God to be a husband of one wife. This would obviously exclude any woman who respects Biblical authority from holding the office of deacon.

    3) Finally, the church has **evangelists**, or preachers (2 Timothy 4:5), who were also under the authority of the elders.

    Adding additional offices or positions within the church is often man's attempt to grasp for

Deacons must be **husbands of only one wife**, and **good managers** of their children and their own households.

- 1 Timothy 3:12

> But you, be sober in all things, endure hardship, do the **work of an evangelist**, fulfill your ministry.
>
> - 2 Timothy 4:5

power or prestige. The Bible speaks nothing of cardinals, nuns, or even youth pastors, and certainly not a Pope—a designation that literally means "Papa" or "Father" to the universal church, the very name Jesus said to "call no man" in Matthew 23:9 because we are to have only one spiritual Father—God. Thus, the office of Pope is far more power than God ever planned for one man to have in the church. Christ alone is the head of the church (Ephesians 5:23).

- Working toward spiritual unity
  In anticipation of His death, the unity of the church was one of the most pressing things on the mind of Christ. He prayed in John 17:20-23, "I do not ask on behalf of these alone, but for those also who believe in Me through their word; that they may all be one; even as You, Father, are in Me and I in You, that they also may be in Us, so that the world may believe that You sent Me. The glory which You have given Me I have given to them, that they may be one, just as We are one; I in them and You in Me, that they may be perfected in unity, so that the world may know that You sent Me, and loved them, even as You have loved Me."

Later, unity was again commanded by God through the apostle Paul when he wrote to the church in Corinth, "Now I exhort you, brethren, by the name of our Lord Jesus Christ, that you all agree and that there be no divisions among you, but that you be made complete in the same mind and in the same judgment" (1 Corinthians 1:10).

Paul begged the Ephesians to be "...diligent to preserve the unity of the Spirit in the bond of peace" (Ephesians 4:1-3).

To restore New Testament Christianity, the church today should not celebrate the division that exists in denominationalism but instead should pursue the unity for which Christ prayed—by jettisoning each and every man-made, extra-Biblical belief and practice and returning to simple, restored, pre-denominational Christianity.

- Pre-denominational Christianity
Another distinguishing characteristic of the church in the New Testament is not being a product of the predicted apostasy (or falling away). It is not one of the denominations (or divisions) that followed this apostasy.

Paul encouraged unity, and as an apostle inspired by God, he was given the ability to see the future divisions that would eventually exist among believers. After spending some time with the church in Ephesus, he then, with a sad heart, warned this flock that "... savage wolves will come in among you, not sparing the flock; and from among your own selves men will arise, speaking perverse things to draw away the disciples after them. Therefore be on the alert, remembering that night and day for a period of three years I did not cease to admonish each one with tears" (Acts 20:29-31). So it was out of pride that men began teaching things that were not true in order to create their *own* following, rather than leading others to humbly follow God.

To explain why anyone would want to have such allegiance to mere men, Paul explains to Timothy, "I solemnly charge you in the presence of God and of Christ Jesus, who is to judge the living and the dead, and by His appearing and His kingdom: preach the word; be ready in season and out of season; reprove, rebuke, exhort, with great patience and instruction. For the time will come when they will not endure sound doctrine; but wanting to have their ears tickled, they will accumulate for themselves teachers in accordance to their own desires, and will turn away their ears from the truth and will turn aside to myths" (2 Timothy 4:1-4). We learn here that

...walk in a manner worthy of the calling with which you have been called, with all humility and gentleness, with patience, showing tolerance for one another in love, being **diligent to preserve the unity** of the Spirit in the bond of peace.

- Ephesians 4:1-3

the reason people would follow such men would be, rather than learning the truth, they wanted to hear a message that would not require them to give up whatever addictive behaviors they desired to keep in their lives. The wanted instead to hear "sweet little lies." Two of these "myths" that were not sound doctrine are specifically mentioned in the following verse. It is certainly no coincidence that the first denomination to come into existence taught both of what God calls here "doctrines of demons."

"But the Spirit explicitly says that in later times some will fall away from the faith, paying attention to deceitful spirits and doctrines of demons, by means of the hypocrisy of liars seared in their own conscience as with a branding iron, men who *forbid marriage* and advocate *abstaining from foods* which God has created to be gratefully shared in by those who believe and know the truth" (1 Timothy 4:1-3). We see the fulfillment of this prediction in history when—although God had mandated a bishop *must* be married (1 Timothy 3:2)—the Pope insisted that a bishop was forbidden to marry. Sadly, it is obvious whose will is most respected in the Catholic church. Also in fulfillment of 1 Timothy 4:3, Paul predicts false teachers would advocate abstaining from foods, and for years Catholics were required to abstain from all meats except fish on Fridays. The Catholic church is a product of this predicted apostasy.

False teachers throughout the early centuries of the church added many other false teachings, from the use of "holy water" to the counting of beads in prayer. So much so that by 1517, Martin Luther, a Catholic monk and teacher, nailed to the church door at Wittenberg, Germany, 95 thesis (propositions for debate) objecting to the practices of the Catholic church. This led to the first major break with Catholicism. Four years later, in 1534, Henry VIII created

An overseer, then, must be above reproach, the **husband of one wife**, temperate, prudent, respectable, hospitable, able to teach...

- 1 Timothy 3:2

the Church of England, from which eventually came the Episcopal church. One year later, the Presbyterian church was established by John Calvin in Switzerland and John Knox in Scotland. John Smythe established the Baptist church in England somewhere between 1607 and 1611, followed by the Congregational church, the United Brethren, and the Methodist church, which was established in England by John and Charles Wesley. Beginning in the 1800s, some, in order to seek followers, began claiming God was speaking to them, including Joseph Smith who began the Mormon Church in 1830 and Ellen G. White who started the Seventh Day Adventist church. Since then, the list has grown to include Christian Science, the Pentecostal churches, the Nazarenes, the Foursquare church, Mennonites, and the Jehovah's Witnesses. Today there are literally thousands of differing churches, and tragically such confusion has hindered many who are trying to find the truth. Still we must continue to work toward fulfilling God's desire for unity. How can this unity be attained? The answer is more simple than our enemy, Satan, would want us to believe.

To strive for the unity prayed for by Jesus, we must first denounce any religious beliefs and teachings that are not given to us by God through His word. We should be able to give a book, chapter, and verse for every religious belief we hold and teach, for it is such false teachings that have caused religious divisions even from the time of the early church—divisions that are not approved of by God. True faith in God is expressed when we trust Him enough to abandon teachings we may have embraced in error. Even when we love the person who taught us this error, we must love God even more (John 14:15). The Lord said, "My sheep hear My voice" (John 10:27). Our encouragement to you is to listen to God, because **He is the only one who will judge us and reward us according**

If you **love Me**, you will keep My commandments.

- John 14:15

to what we have done, whether it be good or bad (Romans 2:6-11). The sooner we begin to believe and accurately teach His word, the sooner we will be prepared for heaven and the sooner we will be in a position to help prepare for heaven the souls of those whom God loves and we love.

The church is intended by God to be a place where we can express our love for Him in the ways He has asked us to express that love. It is a place to have a spiritual family to celebrate with during all your triumphs and joys in life and to be there to support you during the darkest times of your life. The church is a place God has established to help us discover our talents and to use them to improve not only our lives but also the lives of others as we make disciples (Matthew 28:19-20). We learn in the church how to get along with all kinds of people from all kinds of backgrounds with all kinds of personalities, and to—like Jesus—sacrifice our own desires for the good of imperfect people. In the church we grow all the spiritual qualities that give us a happier life now and prepare us to spend an eternity with our heavenly Father.

The church is certainly not the only blessing of being a Christian. In our next and final lesson of this series, we will explore what the Bible says is specifically involved in living a life that is honorable to God, and we will explore many of the blessings we enjoy by choosing such a life.

Living for God's Purposes

What incalculable blessings await those who surrender their lives to God!

Jeremiah 17:7-8 says, "Blessed is the man who trusts in the LORD and whose trust is the LORD. For he will be like a tree planted by the water, that extends its roots by a stream and will not fear when the heat comes; but its leaves will be green, and it will not be anxious in a year of drought nor cease to yield fruit." Like the tree that is fruitful and productive, so is the one who trusts the Lord. It is stable. It is nourished. And because it experiences refreshment, it is then able to benefit others. It fulfils God's purposes for being created and so can we. What a beautiful image.

Christians enjoy the priceless blessing of peace, both now and in eternity. They enjoy freedom from the slavery of sin along with all the cruel consequences of this enslavement, for you have seen for yourself the earthly consequences of living in rebellion to God and how devastating they can be. In contrast, the new Christian enjoys a close and intimate relationship with a merciful heavenly Father who answers prayer and grows, in those who love Him, good character like a fruitful tree.

We love God because He loves us and has rescued us. Psalm 40:2 says, "He lifted me out of the slimy pit, out of the mud and mire; He set my feet on a rock and gave me a firm place to stand." He has rescued us from an eternity in hell. He has given us an incredibly wise guidebook to show us how to live in a way that avoids sin's painful consequences—a book that has shown us how to have a happy marriage and how to successfully raise children.

> Blessed is the man who **trusts in the Lord** and whose trust is the Lord. For he will be like a tree planted by the water, that extends its roots by a stream and **will not fear** when the heat comes; but its leaves will be green, and it will not be anxious in a year of drought nor cease to yield fruit.
>
> - Jeremiah 17:7-8

> He chose us in Him before the foundation of the world, that we would **be holy and blameless** before Him.
>
> - Ephesians 1:4

Besides all this, His followers know the meaning of life—why God created us. Ephesians 1:4 says, "He chose us in Him before the foundation of the world, that we would be holy and blameless before Him." Ephesians 2:10 says, "...we are His workmanship, created in Christ Jesus for good works, which God prepared beforehand so that we would walk in them." What a relief that one does not have to spend one's whole life searching for meaning! Instead, we can spend all that time and effort living out the fulfilling purposes for which we were created.

One Beautiful Motive: Love

Simply put: love and gratitude are by far the only motivations for living the Christian life. When you and I serve God out of gratitude, we will enjoy our lives so much more as Christians. Plus, obeying for the sake of love and gratitude is really the only motivation that opens to us the rewards of obedience. When one is obeying out of guilt, fear, or obligation, such obedience is not from the heart. The truth is, without love for God and deep gratitude for His mercy, our obedience simply will not endure.

- Psalms 103:12 says, "As far as the east is from the west, so far has He removed our transgressions from us." Isn't it really senseless to let our life be driven by such things as past mistakes when we are forgiven utterly? We were not created to carry guilt. Gratitude rather than **guilt** is cleaner fuel to carry us through life.

- It is equally as senseless to let our lives be driven by **resentment**. No matter how we've been wronged in life, we cannot be wronged beyond the wrong of our own sins that cost our heavenly Father the blood of His Son for our forgiveness. Besides, holding onto one's bitterness needlessly complicates current relationships and impedes our own happiness. Resentment, or lack of forgiveness, can even cost you your own forgiveness (Matthew 18:32-33). None of us can afford that. May your life and all you do be motivated by gratitude rather than resentment.

- **Anger** is another emotion that drives far too many people's lives. In contrast, the Christian is told, "...everyone must be quick to hear, slow to speak and slow to anger; for the anger of man does not achieve the righteousness of God" (James 1:19-20). God does not use our anger to help us reach our potential, because anger limits our ability to grow the fruits of the spirit. Pray for God to remove any deeply residing anger from your heart so that your life and all you do can be motivated by gratitude rather than anger.

- Some live their lives based upon **fear**. And yet fear also causes us to miss opportunities to be what God intends us to be, because fear is about self-preservation rather than trusting God to protect us. Ask God for a peace-filled and courageous heart, rather than serving Him from merely a motive of fear.

- In our culture, many are driven by **materialism**. Yet the Christian knows only God is powerful enough to be our security—our one true helper. He is our rock. Longing for more and more can bring dissatisfaction, all the while distracting us from something of much more value—eternal life. According to Proverbs 11:4, "Riches do not profit in the day of wrath, but righteousness delivers from death." A life motivated by gratitude rather than materialism will be truly rich and fulfilling.

- **Social pressure** is yet another empty reason to do what we do. There may come a time in your own life when you must decide whose approval you most desire—your peers' or your Creator's. The moral standards of society will fluctuate, but the Lord's moral standards will not. Galatians 1:10 says, "For am I now seeking the favor of men, or of God? Or am I striving to please men? If I were still trying to please men, I would not

> For am I now seeking the favor of men, or of God? Or am I striving to please men? If I were still **trying to please men**, I would not be a **bond-servant of Christ**.
>
> - Galatians 1:10

...do not be **conformed** to this **world**, but be **transformed** by the **renewing** of your **mind**.

- Romans 12:2

be a bond-servant of Christ." The acceptance of good people will be a by-product of living right—but should not be our primary motivation. Rather than peer pressure, may your life and mine be motivated by a deep love of God and gratitude for all He has done in our lives.

Now that we have discussed proper motivation for following God's will for our lives, let's consider some specifics.

What Are God's Expectations After Baptism?

God desires for us a renewed mind. Romans 12:2 says, "...do not be conformed to this world, but be transformed by the renewing of your mind." Needless to say, renewing one's mind may be the most challenging thing you will ever do, and yet what could be more worthwhile? And just how does one transform one's mind?

- We transform our minds by making an unwavering decision to transform our mind and by depending upon God to give us the strength (1 Peter 4:11) to think differently.

- We transform our minds by nothing less than "taking every thought captive to the obedience of Christ" (2 Corinthians 10:5). Only through prayer and taking control of mental habits can our minds begin to change. God has given us a litmus test of sorts to help us decide what is and what is not spiritually healthy to ponder. "Finally, brethren, whatever is *true*, whatever is *honorable*, whatever is *right*, whatever is *pure*, whatever is *lovely*, whatever is *of good repute*, if there is any *excellence* and if anything *worthy of praise*, dwell on these things" (Philippians 4:8). When a thought comes to you that is counterproductive to your spiritual strength, replace it immediately with another thought that is valuable. Do this consistently, and a new way of thinking will become second nature.

- Also, we transform our minds by setting up an environment for success. "Making no provisions for the flesh with regard to its lusts" (Romans 13:14) helps us maintain our transformed minds. We remove from our lives the influences that make staying faithful to God more difficult.

What is the result of this transformation? When you change your mind, you are *no longer worldly* but instead are able to "present your bodies a living and holy sacrifice, acceptable to God..." (Romans 12:1). Your days will include words and actions that show Christ's love.

God wants an intimate relationship with you. God wants to be first in your heart. Decide to make your Holy Father your best friend. Like all relationships, your relationship with God will be built upon communication. Communicating with God through Bible study and prayer will grow your passion for Him. God speaks to us through His written word, and we speak to Him through prayer. How wonderful that God Himself is willing to listen to all the changes I'd like Him to make to the circumstances around me that are beyond my ability to change—and as if that were not enough, He is willing to use His power to change those things I've requested that are according to His divine will. You will be amazed how much starting and sticking with a daily prayer and Bible reading plan will strengthen you spiritually. You can find Bible reading programs online or often where Christians meet. A few practical ideas related to establishing this habit of daily Bible reading and prayer that you may want to consider include:

a) Use a printed Bible in an accurate translation, like NASV, NKJ, or ESV.

b) Select a time of day and special quiet place for your Bible study and prayer time.

c) Write down discoveries and questions as you read for future study.

...present your bodies a **living and holy sacrifice**, acceptable to God...

- Romans 12:1

d) Prepare for participation in church-organized Bible studies on Sundays and midweek.

e) Write down your prayer requests in a notebook along with things for which you want to praise God or thank Him.

f) As soon as you feel it a possibility, help teach a Bible class. The preparation work will get you digging deeply into God's word.

When you begin reading the Bible regularly, it is best to start in the New Testament. Look for God's will for your life expressed in direct statements or instructions directed to Christians. Look for examples of people doing God's will and obtaining His favor. As you become accustomed to Bible study, you will also become skilled at drawing conclusions (or necessary inferences) by simply using logic. You'll want to purchase a concordance or use a website that has Bible reference materials to help you locate all the verses related to any topic that interests you. Biblegateway.com is a great place to start.

God expects those who are His to live a life of moral integrity. Our friendship with Christ is not unconditional. God can only be in the presence of what is holy, and that is why His children, by the strength He provides, must be holy in order to be His friend (Psalms 5:4; 1 Peter 1:15-16). Yet those who would be God's friends at the same time must become Satan's enemy. And even yielding to a sinful thought begins to give the devil the opportunity to exploit one's weaknesses. When we sin, not only are we hurting ourselves and often others around us, but far more importantly, we are grieving our heavenly Father (Ephesians 4:31).

And just what is moral integrity? Galatians 5:22-23 says when we grow spiritually we exhibit: love, joy, peace, patience, kindness, goodness, faithfulness, gentleness and self-control. In Matthew 5:3-11, Jesus commends the qualities of being humble, merciful, and having a pure heart. We are

> But like the Holy One who called you, **be holy yourselves** also in all your behavior; because it is written, "You shall be holy, for I am holy."
>
> - 1 Peter 1:15-16

commanded in 2 Peter 1:5-7 to add such things as diligence, faith, moral excellence, knowledge, perseverance, godliness, and brotherly kindness to our character. This is what moral integrity looks like. God doesn't care about wealth, beauty, or even intelligence. God cares about character, and when we are serving, we are showing the qualities of selflessness, humility, compassion, love, and kindness. It's not always easy to do the right thing, but it is easier when we remember that the only laws God has given are principles that grant us a happier life presently and in eternity.

In contrast, Galatians 5:19-21 gives us a list of sins—life-ruiners of both the present life as well as the afterlife: "Now the deeds of the flesh are evident, which are: immorality, impurity, sensuality, idolatry, sorcery, enmities, strife, jealousy, outbursts of anger, disputes, dissensions, factions, envying, drunkenness, carousing, and things like these, of which I forewarned you that those who practice such things shall not inherit the kingdom of God." As you compare the fruits of the spirit with the deeds of the flesh, you may notice that the fruits of the spirit directly prevent the deeds of the flesh. God always has a moral replacement for an immoral thought or deed: love prevents strife, joy prevents bitterness, patience prevents anger, peace prevents fear, goodness prevents evil, kindness prevents selfishness. Each fruit of the spirit grows when we react to temptation with a fruit of the Spirit instead of being worried, irritable, disloyal, harsh, or self-indulgent. Every time you defeat a temptation you become more like Christ, and God is honored—which fulfills your purpose for being created. Every time you defeat a temptation you become more practiced for resisting the next, and the consequences of sin are replaced instead with blessings. James 1:12 says, "Blessed is a man who perseveres under trial; for once he has been approved, he will receive the crown of life which the Lord has promised to those who love Him."

...applying all **diligence**, in your **faith** supply **moral excellence**, and in your moral excellence, **knowledge**, and in your knowledge, **self-control**, and in your self-control, **perseverance**, and in your perseverance, **godliness**, and in your godliness, **brotherly kindness**, and in your brotherly kindness, **love**.

- 2 Peter 1:5-7

Now the **deeds of the flesh** are evident, which are: immorality, impurity, sensuality, idolatry, sorcery, enmities, strife, jealousy, outbursts of anger, disputes, dissensions, factions, envying, drunkenness, carousing, and **things like these**...

- Galatians 5:19-21

In 2 Timothy 2:22 we are told to "...flee from youthful lusts and pursue righteousness, faith, love and peace, with those who call on the Lord from a pure heart." The verbs "flee and pursue" remind us that godliness does not "just happen" by accident, it takes intense action and dedication. And the phrase "with those" reminds us of a comforting fact: Christianity is not a lonely endeavor. We can support each other.

Looking more closely at Galatians 5:19-21, note that the expression "and things like these" reveals that this list of sins is not a complete list of all sins. These are really categories of sin that include all sorts of ancient and modern practices.

- For example, the term "immorality" means sexual immorality and includes all sexual sins, including adultery, homosexuality, fornication, incest and pornography. Sins fall in and out of fashion culturally, but God's moral standards do not change.

- The word "impurity" covers much of the same ground, except it condemns the impurity of heart that leads up to the actual sin itself.

- "Sensuality" is defined as "unbridled lust, excess, shamelessness, as in filthy words" or dressing in a way that values fashion over the eternal well being of those trying to keep their hearts and minds clean.

- With respect to "idolatry" one might initially make the mistake of thinking, "Oh, now there's an extinct sin," and yet idolatry is committed any time we place anything or anyone before God: pleasures, hobbies, careers, material possessions and even people—all beneficial things in their proper places—yet each one can sidetrack us and become "idols" above our devotion to God.

- Drunkenness in our culture is typically only associated with alcohol. Yet the Biblical phrase "things like these" would obviously include any chemical that induces intoxication.

Being a faithful Christian is not an easy or effortless task for anyone, including those with a good heart. God expects us to be loyal to Him even while being ridiculed, tempted, and any other time when life is difficult. There are no shortcuts or easy paths to spiritual growth, yet God promises that "No temptation has overtaken you but such as is common to man; and God is faithful, who will not allow you to be tempted beyond what you are able, but with the temptation will provide the way of escape also, so that you will be able to endure it" (1 Corinthians 10:13). And "so that you will not grow weary and lose heart" we are told in Hebrews 12:1-3 that we are being watched by those who have successfully gone on before us. Stop from time to time, especially during periods when your faith is being challenged, and remember those who have gone on in victory before you, for that great cloud of witnesses is watching you. With great interest, they cheer you on as you remove those things from your life that weigh you down spiritually. Like Jesus, we will be challenged to look past our present cross to the joy that is set just on the other side of our distress. Don't lose heart. The same power that made Jesus overcome His ordeal bolsters us when we are weary. We too will "overwhelmingly conquer through Him who loved us" (Romans 8:37).

Life is all about relationships, and part of having moral integrity is nourishing all our relationships. We've discussed how to nourish our relationship with God. Next to God, one of the most important relationships we will ever tend to is our marriage relationship, and one of the important places we must practice our Christianity is within the home. Christians must honor everyone in the family. This is crucial to pleasing God because of how special each person is to God. Notice in the following verse the Lord's recipe for creating a cycle of honor within the home. It may be considered quite

> For consider Him who has **endured such hostility** by sinners against Himself, so that you will **not grow weary** and lose heart.
>
> - Hebrews 12:3

Wives, **be subject** to your own husbands, as to the Lord... Husbands, **love** your wives, just as Christ also loved the church and **gave Himself** up for her...

- Ephesians 5:22, 25

"counter-culture," but it's nonetheless beautiful. "Wives, be subject to your own husbands, as to the Lord. For the husband is the head of the wife, as Christ also is the head of the church, He Himself being the Savior of the body. But as the church is subject to Christ, so also the wives ought to be in their husbands in everything. Husbands, love your wives, just as Christ also loved the church and gave Himself up for her...so husbands ought also to love their own wives as their own bodies. He who loves his own wife loves himself; for no one ever hated his own flesh, but nourishes and cherishes it, just as Christ also does the church" (Ephesians 5:22-30). When a husband nourishes and cherishes his wife to the point he would die for her, and all that he does reflects that love, and a wife in return acknowledges and is grateful for the loving leadership of her husband, a cycle of honor is launched. When husbands give their wives the same consideration, protection, concern and sympathy they extend to themselves, their wives happily follow their lead. A Christian woman realizes that subjection never means inferiority but rather is what her husband needs for his own spiritual growth. The love that holds a marriage together is a sacrificial love, and a husband's headship is not about barking orders but is rather about protecting, nourishing, cherishing, and spiritually preserving (5:23, 26, 29) his wife. Being a husband (or literally "house-band") involves protecting one's wife and children from the spiritual dangers that surround them, and Jesus is asking wives to support their husbands in this important task.

Another relationship God expects us to cultivate is the parent/child relationship.
We are created to love and be loved. People last forever, while careers, projects and possessions are but temporary and have their value only in the fact that those things help sustain our relationships. To invest time into people is to invest time into eternity. Our use of time should reflect this principle, including our parenting. God's recipe

for successful parenting begins in Ephesians 6:1-4 where He says, "Children, obey your parents in the Lord, for this is right. Honor your father and mother (which is the first commandment with a promise), that it may be well with you, and that you may live long on the earth. And, fathers, do not provoke your children to anger; but bring them up in the discipline and instruction of the Lord." The cycle of love in the parent/child relationship then, is that parents—and especially fathers—prayerfully, thoughtfully, and lovingly teach and discipline their children, and children are to respond with heartfelt respect, love, and obedience. This verse points out that it is possible for fathers and mothers to provoke or frustrate their children by being unreasonable, uncaring, or either too harsh or too indulgent. Parents' words and actions must consistently consider the spiritual needs of their children rather than simply venting negative feelings. They need to treat everyone, including their children, the way they would want to be treated (Luke 6:31). God expects children to willingly obey their parents. If you are still growing up and are preparing to leave home to start your own life, understand that while you will eventually be self-directed, the command to honor one's parents never ends (Mark 7:9-11).

What about the Christian's relationship with his or her employer? God expects us to work hard and have a good attitude whether we are in an entry-level position or in upper management. 1 Corinthians 10:31 says, "...whatever you do, do all to the glory of God." We need to make sure that everything we do is consistent with our commitment to honoring God, including while we are in the workplace. Colossians 3:23-24 says, "Whatever you do, do your work heartily, as for the Lord rather than for men, knowing that from the Lord you will receive the reward of the inheritance. It is the Lord Christ whom you serve." Knowing that God is watching us and will reward us for our diligence makes all kinds of work suddenly very

For Moses said, "**Honor your father and your mother**;" and, "He who speaks evil of father or mother, is to be put to death"...

- Mark 7:10

meaningful. Maintaining a good reputation at the workplace may also lead to opportunities to share Christianity with your coworkers.

The last relationship responsibility we will discuss in this lesson is that God expects us to tend to our relationship with the local church. There is a form of worship that is an ongoing, personal dedication to God expressed moment by moment through our holiness, giving up our desires for another, our private prayer life, our service to others, and so on. And there is another form of worship that can only be done collectively with other Christians. One cannot take the place of the other.

Upon baptism, the Lord adds the new Christian to the church that He purchased with His own blood (Acts 2:41, 47; Acts 20:28). While this church includes Christians everywhere, the Bible also teaches that Christians in a specific geographical region are expected to meet, worship and work together. "Let us hold fast the confession of our hope without wavering, for He who promised is faithful; and let us consider how to stimulate one another to love and good deeds, not forsaking our own assembling together, as is the habit of some, but encouraging one another; and all the more as you see the day drawing near" (Hebrews 10:23-25).

What are the blessings and responsibilities of being a member of a congregation? Various acts of worship are placed within the context of the local church, such as:

- The Lord's Supper. This eating of unleavened bread and drinking of the fruit of the vine celebrates and memorializes the death, burial, and resurrection of Jesus Christ. Before I take the Lord's Supper I should take the time to reflect upon my life, renew my commitment to changing where I need to change, and ask God to make me pure again in His sight. It is amazing to realize that the Creator of every tiny creature

So then, those who had received his word were **baptized**; and that day there were **added** about three thousand souls.

- Acts 2:41

visible only by a microscope, the Creator of the vast universe, in fact the Creator of everything, actually wants to meet with you for a cherished moment together weekly. It is wonderful when we recognize that the Lord's Supper is an actual communing with the Lord Himself (Matthew 26:29). In the New Testament the Lord's Supper is something that is only done when Christians assemble (Acts 2:42; 20:7; 1 Corinthians 11:33).

- Likewise, singing is to be done not only to the Lord, but "one to another" (Ephesians 5:19), and according to Colossians 3:16, singing is to "teach and admonish one another." We might create new ways to express our love to our friends, but since God is holy, we express our love to Him in the ways He has given. He has called for singing from our hearts to Him in worship. It is truly awesome that God is willing to listen to the outpouring of our hearts in song as we express our appreciation for the magnificent things He has done in our lives.

- Donating funds (1 Corinthians 16:1-2) is another act of worship, and in the New Testament these funds were exclusively collected at the congregational level, being sent by messengers from the congregation doing the giving (16:3) directly to the ones needing help—an ultra-simplified and ultra-efficient flow of money, free from the costly bureaucracy that too often leads to huge and wasteful church budgets. In the first century, the Lord's church valued using its funds in spreading the word of God and helping needy Christians. This investment trumps wasting money building gymnasiums to play in or paying a big name "Christian band" to come entertain a congregation with a concert.

Another blessing and responsibility of being a member of a congregation is realizing that the church exists so that we accomplish God's work. As we read the New Testament we find that God's work was often accomplished at the

> But I say to you, I will not drink of this **fruit of the vine** from now on until that day when I drink it new **with you** in My Father's kingdom.
>
> - Matthew 26:29

...I came that they may have **life**, and have it **abundantly**.

- John 10:10

local level. Local churches supported preachers (Philippians 4:15); local churches raised funds for benevolence for those near and far (1 Timothy 5:16; 1 Corinthians 16:1-2); and local churches were often the springboards for the gospel (Acts 13:1ff; 1 Timothy 3:15). If you think about it, we as Christians are involved in a cause that is able to solve almost all the world's problems in this life, and in eternity (John 10:10), because living the Christian life prevents or solves a vast variety of problems. As Christians, we have the solution to crime, abortion, gangs, alcoholism, AIDS, divorce, child abuse, poverty, and so on, and that solution is living life according to the instruction manual— the Word of God. Remember, however, that the biggest problem the instruction manual resolves is man's lost condition. The above side benefits are simply the lovely ripple effects of holy living. To help others experience an eternity of bliss rather than damnation exceeds every other act of service we could perform. When you become a Christian, do not automatically cut ties with old friends, rather seek to bring as many friends as possible to Christ, as they see the wonderful changes firsthand in your life as a result of knowing the truth.

Being encouraged and supported by our brothers and sisters in Christ during good times and bad is another blessing of being a member of a local congregation. 1 Corinthians 12:26 says "...if one member suffers, all the members suffer with it; if one member is honored, all the members rejoice with it." Author Rick Warren sums it up well: "A church family identifies you as a genuine believer... moves you out of self-centered isolation...helps you develop spiritual muscle...the body of Christ needs you...you will share in Christ's mission in the world... [the church will] help keep you from backsliding." "Your local fellowship is the place God designed for you to discover, develop, and use your gifts" (*Purpose Driven Life*, pg. 134). "He created the church to meet your five deepest needs: a purpose to live for, people to live with, principles to live by, a profession to live out, and power to live on. There is no other place on earth where you can find all five of these benefits in one place..." Regarding the blessings of participating in the work of the church this author says... "Worship helps you focus on God; fellowship helps you face life's problems; discipleship helps fortify your faith; ministry helps find your talents; evangelism helps fulfill your mission. There is nothing else on earth like the church" (pg. 136)! The church is where your talents can be put to their best use. How do you come to discover what talents you have? In the church you can learn by the feedback of others what your talents are; likewise, in the church it is so important when you recognize a talent in others, become like a mirror, and encourage the growth of their talents.

What should you do if you are asked to do something in your congregation that creates in you tension or discomfort? Do it! Do what you are uncomfortable with so that you will become more comfortable with it over time. Throw yourself into the service areas in which you feel the most at ease, but still do the hard stuff. You'll feel better when your will is stronger than your feelings and you are doing what you should do—not just what you feel like doing. Paul had a great attitude in 2 Corinthians 12:15 when he said, "I will most gladly spend and be expended for your souls."

Another reason God gave us the local church is the blessing of being cared for by the shepherds, or elders of the church. Hebrews 13:17 says, "Obey your leaders and submit to them, for they keep watch over your souls as those who will give an account. Let them do this with joy and not with grief, for this would be unprofitable for you." What can you do to honor your relationship with your elders and be a blessing to them? The first answer is obvious:

- Stay out of sin. Galatians 6:1-2 says when a brother or sister in Christ goes back into sin, "...if anyone is caught in any trespass, you who

> **Obey your leaders** and submit to them, for they keep watch over your souls as those who will give an account. Let them do this with **joy** and not with grief, for this would be unprofitable for you.
>
> - Hebrews 13:17

are spiritual, restore such a one in a spirit of gentleness; each one looking to yourself, so that you too will not be tempted. Bear one another's burdens, and thereby fulfill the law of Christ."

- Be a problem solver, not a problem starter.

- Share your ideas with your elders, then go happily with their judgment calls, even when you think there is a better way of handling things, since they often have much more information they are factoring in as they make their difficult judgment calls.

- Treat them the way you would want to be treated if you were an elder.

- Let the elders know how much you appreciate all they do. Talk them up behind their backs.

And let us consider how to **stimulate** one another to **love** and **good deeds**...

- Hebrews 10:24

Some may ask, "Do I need to attend every worship service?" We must offer ourselves to God not out of fear or duty, but because we deeply love Him. It is important that the new Christian realizes that worship is so much more than simply a ritual. It is an opportunity to express our love to God, to encourage our brethren (Hebrews 10:24), to equip ourselves to resist temptation, to live the Christian life and to teach others (Ephesians 4:11-13). Christians who take advantage of opportunities to learn and grow (Acts 2:42) will be successful (Acts 8:4). Faithful churches of Christ exist throughout this country and far beyond this nation. We have the opportunity of meeting with Christians in other areas when travelling. Our lives will only be that much richer when we alter our plans, as the apostle Paul did in Acts 20:7, to put God first no matter where we happen to be on the first day of the week. No matter what the day of the week, we are told to make the most of our time. And what is the best use of our time? It is including in our daily routine the things that prepare us to give an account of ourselves to God in judgment. As we evaluate our use of time, some things we could ask ourselves may include, "Did today's activities help me fulfill one of God's purposes for my life?" Or, when considering including a new aspect to our lives that will cost us or our families valuable time, "Will this use of my time prepare me or someone else to give an account of our lives to God?" With the proper perspective toward worship, our "Do I need to attend every service?" will be replaced with David's feeling in Psalm 122:1: "I was glad when they said to me, 'Let us go to the house of the LORD.'"

To summarize, being a Christian is about serving God out of the proper motivation—that is, love and gratitude. It is about renewing one's mind and putting God first. Being a Christian is about living a life of moral integrity and nourishing our relationships with God, our spouse, our children, our employer, and the church. **Where do we get the strength to live a life dedicated to accomplishing God's purposes?** Ephesians 3:20-21 answers that question: "Now to Him who is able to do far more abundantly beyond all that we ask or think, according to the power that works within us, to Him be the glory..." God can accomplish through us more than we ever thought possible. 1 Peter 4:11 adds, "...whoever serves is to do so as one who is serving by the strength which God supplies; so that in all things God may be glorified." God will give us the strength we need to live a life dedicated to accomplishing His purposes. And how is this strength accessed? God's strength is accessed by asking Him for it in prayer and keeping that line of communication open by our faithfulness (Luke 21:36, 1 Peter 3:7)

Let's conclude our series with three beautiful promises from God for those who would serve Him:

"Listen to Me, O house of Jacob, and all the remnant of the house of Israel, you who have been borne by Me from birth and have been carried from the womb; even to your old age I will be the same, and even to your graying years I will bear you! I have done it, and I will carry you; and I will bear you and I will deliver you" (Isaiah 46:3-4). If this was God's

> I was **glad** when they said to me, "Let us go to the **house of the Lord**."
>
> - Psalm 122:1

relationship with physical Israel, how much more do these intimate and comforting words belong to spiritual Israel, composed of those who have the faith of Abraham, whose hearts are fully God's? What a connection. What nurturing. What gratitude we have for His comfort. If you have not done so already, we invite you to become a blessed child of God.

In Psalm 16:11 David says to God, "In Your presence is fullness of joy; In Your right hand there are pleasures forever."

To God's faithful children, it will on the final day be said, "Well done, good and faithful servant; you have been faithful over a little, I will set you over much; enter into the joy of your master" (Matthew 25:21-22).

This writer's prayer is that the readers of this series will hear those most precious words as they enter an eternity basking in the glory of His Holiness. Amen.

18341084R00042

Made in the USA
San Bernardino, CA
21 December 2018